Computers

Acquisitions Editor: Jodi McPherson
Editor-in-Chief: Natalie Anderson
Project Manager (Editorial): Eileen Clark
Editorial Assistant: Jodi Bolognese
Senior Marketing Manager: Emily Knight
Marketing Assistant: Scott Patterson
Production, Manager (Production): Digital Content Factory
Project Manager (Production): Digital Content Factory
Associate Director, Manufacturing: Vincent Scelta
Manufacturing Buyer: Lynne Breitfeller
Design Manager: Digital Content Factory
Designer: Digital Content Factory
Composition: Digital Content Factory

Pearson Education LTD.
Pearson Education Australia PTY, Limited
Pearson Education Singapore, Pte. Ltd
Pearson Education North Asia Ltd
Pearson Education, Canada, Ltd
Pearson Educación de Mexico, S.A. de C.V.
Pearson Education-Japan
Pearson Education Malaysia, Pte. Ltd

10 9 8 7 6 5 4
ISBN 0-13-145195-2

Contents

COMPUTER TECHNOLOGY
Education

- A Framework for Education, Present and Future

- Connecting America's Classrooms

- Administrative applications

- Online Resources

- Online Learning

- Programming and Education

- Computers in Training for Business and Industry

A Framework for Education, Present and Future

Computer technology is helping to provide an excellent framework that extends the resources available to education. The computer workstation, the Internet, and specialized software are all being used more and more in education to provide tools and resources both in the classroom and outside it.

Administrative tools, interactivity, and improved access to information and peers, are benefits that students and teachers alike are gaining by incorporating computers into education. From computer-assisted instruction to complete schools online, to project and grade management software, computers are creating a framework that is not changing education, but supporting it.

Vision of Education in 2020

But before examining the role of computer technology in education now, a better way to illustrate its impact would be to try to imagine what education might be like in the year 2020. That is what Randy Hinrichs, Manager of Microsoft Research Learning Science and Technology Group, has done in a white paper entitled "A Vision for Life Long Learning - Year 2020". In the paper, Hinrichs examines computer technology in education at five stages in life: from birth, prior to school, in elementary school, in high school, and during college and professional education afterwards.

From birth, children will play with toys that are programmed to record and analyze their interactions, which allows the toy to provide the parents with feedback on the child's progress, so that they can guide his or her learning.

For the pre-school child, learning will take the shape of truly 3-D virtual reality games, to help promote reading, writing, mathematical and motor skills. The games' software again monitors the child's progress, and individualizes the games to meet the child's needs and preferences. Parental interaction also helps shape the learning content and keep parents informed and in control of the subject matter.

During the early years of school, computer technology will link children into learning groups, regardless of geography. Using networking communication technologies, children will learn to work together to solve problems and complete projects. Technology embedded in the learning tools will continue to monitor the child's progress and measures performance.

This type of learning technology that constantly monitors the child's progress takes the form of a virtual mentor, an interactive construct that, in addition to monitoring progress, guides the student in their learning, answers their questions, and establishes a dialogue with them to assess their emotions and competencies. This mentor software will accompany the student throughout their life, alternating between the roles of counselor, teacher's assistant, or personal assistant as needed.

In high school, the student works on more practical, hands-on projects, with networked access to experts and teachers whenever needed. The virtual-reality teaching tools used, similar to the toys of childhood, analyze the student's learning habits and styles. In conjunction with the virtual mentor, these learning tools modify themselves to suit the student's learning styles and education goals.

Throughout the whole learning process, most computer input is provided through voice commands. Any data resulting from interactions with other computing devices, such as video conferencing, digital lectures, and collaborative tools is recorded and saved so that the student can go back and review or study any of their academic interactions whenever they need to. This information will be saved for life, and through ubiquitous network devices, the student will have access to that information at any time in the future. Learning is never forgotten even when not practiced, because students can re-immerse themselves in the content, on demand.

The impact of current and emerging technologies on the classroom and education in the year 2020

So where do today's emerging technologies fit into this vision of future classrooms? The Internet already makes expert knowledge about certain subjects immediately available to classrooms. Video conferencing, collaborative work with remote students, and multimedia records of learning experiences are already a reality, even if the technology is still in its infancy. Students already grow familiar with computers from a very young age, so the technology is becoming less and less an end in itself, requiring a high learning curve, and more an intuitive tool with which to apply learning, as integral as pencil and paper.

A Laptop for Every 7th Grader

In 2002, the state of Maine signed a $37.2-million contract with Apple computers to purchase an iBook laptop for every seventh- and eighth- grade public school student and teacher in the state. Wireless networks are to be installed in every school with classes using the laptops, so that students can network with each other and with the Internet while sitting at their desks.

The program began in March 2002 in nine demonstration schools, where potential problems could be worked out and advantages studied prior to the full roll-out of the program in late 2002 and throughout 2003. By the fall of 2002, 18,000 laptops had been delivered to students and teachers across the state.

Many teachers saw results immediately. Students who previously had handwriting problems were able to turn in completely legible assignments. Other teachers reported that students who normally showed no interest in class at all were very engaged by the work on the laptops and were excited to return to class. Ways in which the teachers had students put the laptops to good use included: collecting data and making graphs for math assignments; writing papers, journaling or carrying out literary research in language arts; researching and "buying" stocks; researching and reporting on native American tribes, reading about current events online and researching current issues for social studies classes; or collecting experimental data, documenting data with graphs, writing lab reports and creating slide-show presentations for science classes.

There were pitfalls, of course. At the beginning of the program, many teachers were far less familiar with computers than their students were. The state provided only two days of training for all teachers at the beginning of the program, and many of those with little computing experience felt this was inadequate. They complained that it was taking them a lot of extra time to work the unfamiliar technology into their lessons.

Most schools do not let the students take the laptops home, concentrating instead on ways in which the students can use the laptops in the classroom. Teachers also have software on their laptops that allows them to see the screen of any student computer, when it is turned on. In this way, students truly did use the laptops for scholastic purposes only.

The program is still under way, with plans to review it after all the laptops have been delivered. Many questions raised have yet to be answered, though. In particular, how prepared will high schools be in 2004 and 2005 when they receive the previous year's grade eight students, who by then will have spent one or even two years learning in such a hands-on computing environment?

Connecting America's Classrooms

The vision of education in 2020 sees classroom boundaries removed entirely by global networks, where students can learn together no matter where they live in the world. That is nowhere near a reality today, but Internet access for schools is rapidly becoming a necessity rather than a luxury.

Current State of Connectivity in America's Schools

According to the document "Internet Access in U.S. Public Schools and Classrooms: 1994-2001", released in September 2002 by the US Department of Education's National Center for Education Statistics (NCES), as of fall 2001, 99 percent of U.S. public schools had access to the Internet, and 87 percent of instructional rooms in public schools had Internet access. Compare this to the NCES's first study in 1994, where it was reported that only 35 per cent had access.

The speed and constancy of the Internet connections, according to the study, are fairly high: in 2001, 85 percent of public schools had broad band Internet connections.

Most importantly, the ratio of students to computers in 2001 was 5.4 to 1. This is a great improvement over the original statistic of 12.1 to 1, in 1998. Most experts consider a ratio of 4-5 students per computer to be acceptable for effective use in education.

Consortium for School Networking

The Consortium for School Networking (CoSN) is a national non-profit organization devoted to promoting the use of information technologies and the Internet for the improvement of learning, from kindergarten to grade 12.

The consortium works in many ways to achieve this goal. First, it organizes developmental activities aimed at helping school leaders at all levels (national, state, and local) to make sure that technology has a positive impact on learning. It also promotes awareness of emerging technologies, to help schools make the most of the best tools for computer learning environments.

The CoSN also provides advocacy for technology-related issues. For example, in 2003, many states as well as the federal government launched inquiries into the E-rate program for school discounts on telecommunication services, after cases of mismanagement and misappropriation of funds were discovered. Some politicians even proposed cutting off the program completely. The CoSN provided information and advocacy at several levels of government, defending the E-rate program. The result: the FCC announced in April 2003 that it will streamline the E-rate program instead of cutting it.

Computers in the Classroom

The computer will never be a replacement for the teacher in the classroom, but as a multimedia platform for showcasing concepts, it excels. From creating lessons on PowerPoint presentations to running software designed for specific tutorials or for testing in the classroom, the computer is really proving its worth, especially when it comes to saving time. With classroom testing, for example, students can take a test and learn the results as soon as they have finished.

Interactive simulations

Computer simulations are very cost-effective ways to reproduce phenomena in the classroom. For example, computer slide shows or computer-generated dissections have been popular in science classrooms for a while now, especially in cases where the materials for the dissection are not available.

Taking dissection a step further in higher education, certain institutions are using virtual reality to simulate dissections. In Canada, for example, the University of Calgary has a $6 million virtual reality room using the CAVE automatic virtual environment technology. The CAVE is a 2.5-cubic-meter room, where four projectors display representations of the human body on the walls. This, combined with the use of a special pair of glasses, creates a very convincing and detailed 3-D image, as though the viewer were actually inside whatever is being projected.

A project by the National Library of Medicine called the Visible Human Project has undertaken to create 3-D image files of the entire human body, piece by piece and layer by layer. With these images loaded into the CAVE unit in Calgary, students can literally move through the highly detailed simulation, getting a much better understanding of the anatomy than the destructive process of dissection allows.

Challenges to Widespread Adoption

The challenges to widespread adoption of computers in the classroom is, as always, limited to two main obstacles, funds and experience.

Many public schools are already cash-strapped to begin with, so the purchase of enough computer systems to meet the 4-5 computers-per-student ratio is simply out of the question. In some cases, where schools have trouble meeting the monetary demands for even the most basic facilities like books or desks, finding the capital to purchase computers often takes a back seat.

There is also the matter of teacher experience with computers. In many instances, students are more familiar with computers than their teachers. It is extremely hard for teachers to take the time and effort to work computer activities into their curriculum when they simply don't have the computer knowledge to do so.

Administrative applications

The computer's first role has always been as an organizational tool for data, and in the work of a teacher there is no lack of data to organize. But educators can do much more than simply record grades or print lesson plans. Classroom data can be analyzed for trends.

Managing Instruction

Applications abound that have been produced specifically to help teachers create and maintain lesson plans. Most of these applications will have other useful and related functions, such as managing grades, assignments and organizing lesson calendars. ThinkWave Educator is one example of this type of software.

Testing

With national standards and standards testing such an important part of the current education system, computers are proving their worth time and time again. Exams based on national standards can in many cases be graded by computer, keeping the results turnaround time to a minimum. Prior to the use of computers for testing, a standardized exam written in May might not return results to the teacher until October. At this point, it is too late to help students failing in certain areas, since by then they have already moved on to a different teacher. With computer testing and grading, results can be produced almost instantly.

Communicating with Parents

The Internet plays a huge role in facilitating contact between parents and schools. Almost all schools maintain at least a minimal Web site, which is used to communicate announcements and school news to parents. E-mail is another tool that cannot be overlooked in its ability to allow dialogue between parents and teachers, or between parents and the school administration. Some school districts, for example, Carlisle Area school district in Pennsylvania, are even implementing initiatives where parents can log on to Web sites and access student grades and teacher comments.

MIT Thinking Tags

MIT researchers in technology and education have developed a concept called Thinking Tags, for exploring and studying relationships. The Thinking Tag is a circuit board "name tag", with five small LEDs, some color-coded buttons, and a number. The behavior of the tag's LEDs is controlled by a single computer, with instructions sent to the tags by radio signals, as well as from tag to tag via infrared transmitters. One highly educational activity for the students is to use tags to study the spread and behavior of a virus.

The students wear the tags and walk around a room, socializing with each other. At a certain point, various tags will start lighting up, indicating that the wearer has been infected with a virus.

At this point, the students examine each other's tags to find out which tags were infected by the "virus" and why, as well as to try to determine where the "outbreak" began. They will examine factors such as the color of the buttons on the tags, who spoke with whom, and which LEDs lit up when infected.

Through trial and error (for example, by having a certain person turn off their tag and sit out during an experiment), the students will determine what the characteristics of the virus are, how it was spread, and where it began.

The advantage of these experiments is that the participating students don't necessarily need to have a lot of technical knowledge. As well, the experiments can succeed only if all the students work together, which encourages productive interaction and group effort.

Online Resources

Simply having computers and knowing how to use them is not enough for truly effective integration of computer technology in the classroom. A computer loaded with the latest in educational software is still a blank canvas. The student, as well as the instructor, needs direction and content.

Fortunately, there are many resources, online and offline, for both students and teachers.

Student Resources

For students, the biggest resource of all is obvious enough: the World Wide Web. Sites abound with information and knowledge on just about any subject a student can be expected to research. It almost goes without saying that the Internet is the best source for up-to-the-minute news. There are also many services offered online dedicated to research: even the venerable Encyclopedia Britannica has an online subscription service that gives members access to all its most current encyclopedia articles and multimedia presentations. Microsoft Encarta is another online encyclopedia aimed specifically at school students.

The International Children's Digital Library

Encyclopedias and news sites are not all the Internet has to offer for schoolchildren. Thanks to a project by the University of Maryland funded by the National Science Foundation and the Institute for Museum and Library Services, a free online library of children's books from all over the world is being established online, called the International Children's Digital Library (ICDL). The ICDL has several goals:

- To collect more than 10,000 books online from at least 100 different languages.
- To present this all in an interface that has been designed with input from children, in order to make reading these books as easy and as inviting as possible.
- To study the concepts of rights' management in the digital age, the impact that access to digital material has on school programming and libraries, and children's attitudes towards other cultures as a result of access to this library.

The interface for reading books was developed with input from children of all different ages, and resulted in the creation of several different views, from a single-page view to a double-page view or a spiral-page view that allows a child to navigate an entire book quickly and intuitively.

When searching for books, children can navigate by color, shape or format, or by the way the book might make them feel. They can also search by clicking on a picture of a globe to select a book's place of origin. The search interface is entirely visual, to make it as easy-to-use as possible for children still learning to read.

The program hopes the project will bring children's literature to areas where literature in a child's language is hard to find, or where books themselves are rare. "There are places in outer Mongolia where you will see a computer connected to the Internet faster than you will ever see a great library or a great bookstore.", says Jane White, project director.

Teacher Resources

Naturally, teachers can make use of the same informational resources that students use, especially if using those resources will be made part of a particular lesson or class. But teachers are also using the Internet as a means of networking with other teachers, to do everything from sharing information and lesson plans to creating new ways of teaching old content. The following are three examples of the type of resources teachers can find, specifically designed for teachers.

ERIC, the Educational Resources Information Center, is a national information system for educators, to provide access to education literature and resources. The ERIC archives can be accessed on the World Wide Web or on CD-ROM. Ask ERIC is a personalized Internet-based service for accessing the ERIC database. Educators needing to know the latest information on education, curriculum or development can submit their question through the AskEric.org Web site, and an answer will be researched and e-mailed back within two business days. The Web site also provides access to archives of questions already asked, complete with citations and links to articles in the ERIC database as well as links to other related sources on the Internet.

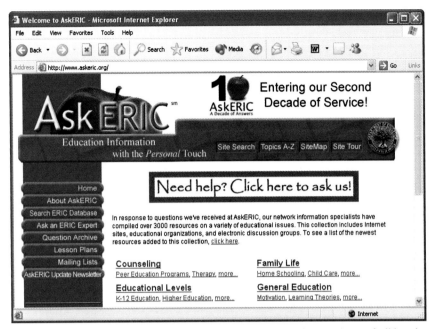

Fig. 1.1 The AskERIC Web site, a handy online resource for teachers of all levels.

The Web-based Inquiry Science Environment (WISE) is an online learning environment created to teach science in a way that differs from the traditional classroom lessons. Following the WISE curriculum, students instead log on to a Web site to be assigned activities, take part in peer discussion groups, create maps and graphs based on data collected in the activities, and find links to further information. The WISE curriculum is designed to meet current national standards, and covers current scientific topics such as genetically modified foods or earthquake prediction. The main learning goal behind WISE is to encourage students to work independently when learning. WISE.

Another project that is all about sharing information is the MIT OpenCourseWare project. Through the project, MIT is publishing course information openly on the Web, making it freely available for anyone. This course information includes course summaries, syllabuses, lesson plans, lecture notes, and even videos of lectures when available. The institution hopes that prospective students will benefit from this information by using it to evaluate MIT courses, that teachers from other institutions can use it to supplement their own courses, or that people carrying out self-study programs can use it to guide their studies. The OpenCourseWare project is NOT a distance learning program that will earn anyone credit or degrees from MIT, but simply an attempt to share information for the sake of sharing knowledge. Course topics available range from Aeronautics and Astronautics, to History, to Cognitive Sciences.

The Role of the Teacher

Despite many initial misgivings, adoption of computer technology in education has not made the teacher obsolete. In fact, use of technology in the classroom demands the intervention of the teacher more than ever. However, the teacher's role has changed in a small but important way: pushing aside the stereotypical role of the orator who drills knowledge into the heads of their students, technology allows the teacher to step into the role of enabler.

As Jim Slotta, project director for the WISE science environment project (see above) puts it: teachers can use computer technology to "move from being the sage on the stage to a guide on the side". By using the engaging and pro-active aspects of computer technology to help guide students towards making their own decisions and coming up with their own answers, teachers can change the way they help students learn.

Teacher training

But first, teachers need to be sufficiently comfortable with computer technology to alter their curriculum and the way in which they deliver it. The question remains: on whom does the responsibility fall to ensure that teachers receive the training they need to use it?

Teachers can in some cases turn to the school administrations and school districts for training. Gold School District 67, in Morton Grove, Illinois, is a small school district that has implemented a technology training program for the teachers in the district. Three years in length, the "Golf Academy" (as it is called) comprises 36 hours of intensive training, 12 of which are carried out during two weeks in the summer. Teachers are not paid for this time, but that doesn't stop them from enrolling.

The program is small (only eight teachers per class), but start-up costs are marginal and the range of topics covered over the three years of training is extensive. The first year covers basics like word processing and spreadsheets. The second year involves building on those skills to communicate and organize information using various media tools such as scanners, digital cameras or the Internet. Year three covers ways to integrate those new tools into the classroom.

Peer mentoring is also common. Many online sites exist where teachers can discuss with other teachers their ideas involving technology. Some districts also have organized programs for encouraging peer help. For instance, to help grade seven and eight teachers make full use of the new laptops in in Maine schools, the state chose certain teachers with more computer experience to work as regional integration mentors (RIMs) to help others get comfortable with the technology and work it into the classroom.

Costs of Technology in Education

No doubt about it, computer technology can be used to improve the quality of education. But does the public education system have the money to afford to be cutting edge?

The problem, of course, lies with the furious pace of development in the computer industry. It is very difficult to keep on top of the latest innovations for learning when the computer hardware requirements for certain software become more demanding every single year.

But more importantly, the challenge lies in producing the funds to purchase the technology in the first place. With public school districts forced to make recent massive budget cuts (for example, in 2002 alone, the state of Indiana cut $500 million from the K-12 education budget, the Los Angeles Unified school district cut $428.5 million from their budget, and even the small town of Neenah, Wisconsin, found it had to cut $1.5 million from its school budget - its first education cuts in 20 years), funds for new technology have been hit hard.

Programs like the state of Maine's grade seven and eight laptop initiative cost $37.2 million. This money came from a budget surplus that the state chose to apply to this groundbreaking project. But budget surpluses are few and far between during the current economic recession, and as one-time expenditures, cannot be depended on.

Grassroots technology initiatives are often more affordable, like the Golf School District's Golf Academy, which has a budget of $25,000. However, programs like this are small scale (eight teachers per year), and when scaled up, the prices once again start to become prohibitive.

Advocates of computer technology in education find themselves constantly fighting a hard battle against the bottom line, and the return on investment with this type of spending is difficult to quantify. However, with the focus on national educational standards, individual student results are becoming easier to quantify. This means more research on the effect of computer technology in education, and it becomes easier to pinpoint where computers are making an impact on learning and grades.

Online Learning

Considering the Internet's great capacity for increased communication and sharing knowledge, it wasn't too much of a stretch to transpose the concept of distance learning to the Internet. In fact, the richness of media on the Internet and the potential for many forms of communication have made it an ideal space in which to provide distance learning.

Distance Education

By now, the concept of education over the Internet has caught on so firmly that the question is not "Is it possible to find distance education online?", but rather "What schooling do I want to learn online?"

Online schools exist for all levels of learning, some of which are schools offering online supplements to their existing in-school classes, while others are 100% virtual schools, with no brick and mortar classrooms at all. Online schooling exists for levels from kindergarten (schools like the Western Pennsylvania Cyber Charter School) all the way to university-level programs - even a law school like the Concord Law School, which exists only on the Internet.

University of Phoenix, MBA programs

The University of Phoenix, a private university, was one of the first accredited universities to offer complete undergraduate and graduate programs over the Internet. It is especially well-known for its Master of Business Administration (MBA) program. The classes are offered one at a time, and are five to six weeks in length, which allows the student to go at their own pace while working a full-time job. The program takes roughly two to three years to complete.

Lectures, questions, and assignments are retrieved online, and downloaded for offline review later. The university offers a toll-free technical support line for students, so help is never far away if things are not working properly. All the school-related administrative activities the student might need to do can be carried out online through the university's Web site: registration, payment, purchasing books, viewing grades and credit status, requesting transcripts, etc.

The University of Phoenix also has classrooms in 26 states, as well as in Puerto Rico and Vancouver, Canada, and offers flexible part-classroom, part-online schooling for those students in areas that have real campuses.

Concord Law School, Online School of Law

In November 2002, the Concord Law School, an exclusively online school of law, graduated its first class of Juris Doctorates. The class, consisting of 14 graduates, is a testament to the relatively new concept of studying law using the Internet .

The school offers its classes in the three-year law program using e-mail, streamed video lectures, student debates in forums on the school's Web site, and real-time online multiple-choice tests. The appeal is beginning to grow, with over 1,100 students from 12 different countries studying in the program as of 2002.

The largest hurdle that Concord has had to overcome is official recognition. The American Bar Association has not yet granted the institute full accreditation, though it has permitted law students certain credits for courses taken through Concord or other distance learning programs. Currently, if Concord law students want to practice law, the only state in which they can work is California (which doesn't require law students to have attended an accredited institution before taking the bar exam).

Virtual Reality

Virtual reality is still a long way from Microsoft's vision of completely immersive virtual lessons. Instead, it is used today mostly as a supplement to existing lesson materials, a way to provide a different vantage point on certain topics. For instance, many education sites (such as National Geographic Education) and many of America's national parks (such as Yellowstone) have virtual reality tours available online.

Programming and Education

Teaching younger students to write computer programs was merely a tool used for educational research, until the explosion of personal computer use in the 1980s, with the introduction of popular, affordable computers like the Apple. Simplified programming languages, like Logo or BASIC, became easy to use and teach in the classroom, given that computers were now accessible to the general public.

Learning Basic Programming Concepts

Teaching young students how to write computer programs is invaluable as a learning tool. Programming concepts are important not only to students wishing to learn to program, but to the non-programmer as well, since it teaches:

- Critical thinking.
  Programming requires planning and analysis of the goal to be achieved in order to be successful.
- Practical problem solving.
  With the constraints imposed by a computer programming language, students learn to find creative solutions for solving practical problems and realizing concrete goals, like animating a turtle or drawing graphics, for example.
- Cooperative learning.
  Some students will learn and master aspects of a programming language at a different pace than others. Working together towards the common goal of building a certain program requires students to share knowledge and collaborate productively.

Using Logo as a Teaching Tool

Logo is both a simplified programming language and environment used to teach programming concepts to children, as well as an educational philosophy that uses programming to reinforce traditional scholastic concepts.

Logo is continually evolving (it was first created in 1967 by researchers at MIT) to take advantage of each new computing technology as it becomes available (computers today are very different from computers in 1967, obviously). It is essentially an environment, run on a computer, that recognizes a simplified computing language. The language used in Logo programs is simple and clear, which makes it easy to learn even for younger children. Yet it also incorporates current programming concepts and syntax, making it a "real" programming language.

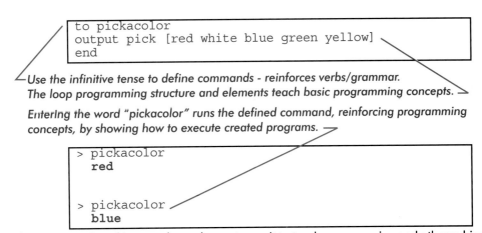

```
to pickacolor
output pick [red white blue green yellow]
end
```

Use the infinitive tense to define commands - reinforces verbs/grammar.
The loop programming structure and elements teach basic programming concepts.

Entering the word "pickacolor" runs the defined command, reinforcing programming concepts, by showing how to execute created programs.

```
> pickacolor
red

> pickacolor
blue
```

Fig. 1.2 Examples of Logo code, and ways to use it to teach programming and other subjects.

One of the more popular current versions of Logo in American schools is MicroWorlds Pro, by Logo Computer Systems Inc. (LCSI). In addition to providing the environment for Logo, LCSI also sells pre-made Logo tools specifically tailored for certain learning goals, such as EnrichedMath (to teach mathematics concepts to grades 5-8 through programming) or JournalZone (in which students write and publish their own online multimedia journals).

Specialized Applications

Many specialized applications also find their way into education, from servers dedicated to creating environments where students can collaborate remotely, to creating new ways for physically-challenged users to access computers (and thus use them to learn).

Team Projects - Collaborative Writing

The school of management at the University of Massachusetts-Amherst uses Microsoft SharePoint server (part of Office XP) to store all core curriculum material for students, who previously were paying over $100 per course per year on textbooks. SharePoint also enables students to work on more career-type exercises, for example, collaborative exercises involving online research to resolve business-related problems.

Resources for the Physically Challenged

"Give me a lever long enough and a place to stand, and I will move the world" said the Greek philosopher, Archimedes. The Archimedes Project, an independent research organization at Stanford University, is dedicated to making computer technology the lever that allows physically challenged people to move their world.

The current main goal of the Archimedes Project is to develop tools that grant universal access to computers to physically challenged users. Instead of taking an existing computer and adapting it to the user's specific abilities, they design tools that can be used with any computer or computer-based device. In 2002, the Archimedes Project released a product called the Natural Input Platform (NIP), which uses voice recognition to send commands to a computer, for people who are visually impaired or who have limited motor control.

Another new technology that is finding its way into computer access for the physically challenged is haptics. Haptics is the technology of the sense of touch. A project by Certec at Lund University in Sweden uses a haptic device called the PhANTOM to allow visually impaired users to navigate around the Windows operating system by feel. The haptic device applies pressure to the user's finger to simulate what the user is touching on the screen.

Career Opportunities

Naturally, knowing computer technology has always been a boon for job-seeking teachers, and is a skill worth having. But as in many other parts of industry, the real technological advancement has come from the Internet and the way it is used to connect people from all over the country and all over the world.

Newly graduated education students and experienced teachers alike can find many career opportunities online. The market is wide open for new educational resources to be developed for the World Wide Web.

Another breakthrough for job-seeking teachers (as well as job-seekers in any discipline, for that matter) has been online job search portals, such as Monster.com. These huge databases of job listings allow job-seekers to find and apply for jobs in other parts of the country (or even the world), that they simply wouldn't have found locally.

Computers and Literacy

A National Reading Panel Report of March 2000 identified research trends indicating that computer technology is an effective tool for teaching reading. Not only because reading is essential to be able to use many aspects of the computer, but also because technology is a way to encourage struggling students to work harder on their literacy - just the possibility of learning to operate the computer is often incentive enough to stimulate a frustrated student's interest.

Findings by the same panel indicate that using word processors to teach literacy is beneficial because reading instruction is more effective when combined with writing instruction.

Computers in Training for Business and Industry

It almost goes without saying that the impact computer technology has had on elementary, secondary, and post-secondary education is just as valid in the corporate education and training sectors. Specifically, though, businesses need specialized training that ensures their staff are studying only the skill sets needed for their work, and ways to certify that a skill set is sufficient for their business.

Certification Training and Assessment

In the past, a college or university's reputation has always been enough to vouch for the quality of the education received by graduates. But when computer skills began to be a requirement for jobs, employers have had no frame of reference for evaluating an applicant's computer skills.

Enter computer standards certifications. Organizations like the Computing Technology Industry Association (CompTIA) were founded to established an industry-created series of certifications, based on standards required for the industry. CompTIA's famous A+ certification, for instance, evaluates the skills necessary for an entry-level computer technician. Because the certification standards are established by industry leaders and made public knowledge, employers who see that an applicant has achieved their A+ certification can be assured that the job candidate has the necessary skills to do tasks at that level. CompTIA has established certification standards for many other computer-related disciplines, too: Network+ for administrating networks; Linux+ for installing, maintaining, and administering Linux networks; or IT Project+ for the technical and soft skills necessary to manage IT projects - just to name a few.

Just-in-time and Web-based learning

Many businesses have a hard time balancing the need to upgrade employee skills and staying focussed on meeting aggressive goals. This has evolved into a market for what is known as "just-in-time learning", where a user undergoes intensive training to acquire a specific skill when that skill becomes necessary for their work.

Online learning, especially Web-based courses, are becoming the delivery method of choice for corporate just-in-time learning. Online technical training providers, such as NETg, offer courses that teach towards various vendor and standard certifications, such as Microsoft's MCSE, or CompTIA's A+,

What makes this kind of training "just-in-time" is that students can take assessment tests prior to starting a course. The assessment identifies what skills the student already has and where they require training, and then identifies the areas where the student needs to study. By taking only the modules that teach skills they haven't yet mastered, a student can drastically cut the time needed for training.

2

COMPUTER TECHNOLOGY in
Science & Medicine

- Overview
- Disease Control
- Genetic Research
- Portable Technology
- Medical Imaging
- Medical Advice and Databases
- Telemedicine
- Technology and Disabilities
- Artificial Intelligence in Medicine

Overview

Advances in technology continue to push advances in medicine, both in medical research and in the development of new applications for health care. The mapping of the human genome would not have been possible without the use of the sophisticated computers now available. This event alone is expected to spark a quantum leap in medical research, diagnosis and the introduction of new treatments for years to come.

As computing technology compresses more power into smaller packages, the doors are opened for new applications. For example, miniature digital video cameras could be ingested (in pill form) to provide video images inside the digestive system, potentially avoiding invasive exploratory surgery.

Technology is being applied to all areas of health care. In health administration, systems are being used to reduce the administrative and paper burden, and to reduce cost. Lower administration costs can free up funds for patient services or reduce overall costs. Technology is being applied in diagnostic services to improve accuracy and to provide earlier diagnosis and treatment. And while there are many new applications and technologies being developed, there are many legal, regulatory and ethical challenges that need to be addressed.

Kaiser Permanente, the largest health-care group in the U.S., plans to adopt an automated medical record system for its 30 medical centers and over 400 medical offices. This represents 8.4 million members and 11,000 physicians. By eliminating current paper-based systems and integrating disparate systems through an integrated data repository, the system will reduce administrative costs and errors resulting from the paper-based systems, as well as improve efficiency and patient safety.

Disease Control

Computer technology plays an enormous role in disease control today, especially in cases of world-wide epidemics, as in the recent outbreak of Severe Acute Respiratory Syndrome (SARS).

WHO and SARS

Originating in China in November of 2002, the then unknown disease, later named SARS, had spread quietly and quickly throughout Asia by early March of 2003.

The World Health Organization (WHO) uses computer network technology in several ways in the control of infectious diseases.

First, the WHO employs a tool called the Global Public Health Intelligence Network (GPHIN), which is a customized search engine that continuously scans the Internet world wide for rumors and reports of suspicious disease activity. The information collected by this search engine is then organized by computer and reviewed and filtered by humans to be catalogued or potentially flagged for further investigation. It is thanks to this system that the WHO first started monitoring the emergence of the disease in November 2002, despite the Chinese government's attempt to conceal their efforts to control the disease. The service also helps the WHO keep track of false rumors, so that they can quickly be refuted before any public damage is caused.

In March, the WHO scaled up its response to the growing SARS epidemic, and established a global network that consisted of 11 leading laboratories which, through information shared on a secure Web site and via round-the-clock teleconferencing, collaborated to work on identifying the virus and to develop a reliable test for potentially-infected patients.

Thanks to this effort, exactly a month after it was established, two members of the network (the Centers for Disease Control in the U.S. and the BC Cancer Agency in Canada) announced that they had successfully sequenced the SARS genome. The genome sequences confirmed it as a coronavirus, by showing similarities between it and other coronavirii known to infect pigs and poultry. Based on this genetic knowledge, the reliability of tests for suspected cases of SARS was increased, and hospitals and health-care organizations developed better measures for isolating and treating the disease. On July 5, 2003, the World Health Organization officially announced that SARS had been contained, with 20 days having passed since the last reported case.

Genetic Research

The U.S. Human Genome Project began in 1990 and was expected to take 15 years. With advances in technology and the cooperation of the world-wide scientific community, the project will be completed in 2003. The goals of the project were to identify all 30,000 genes in human DNA, determine the sequences of the 3 billion chemical-base pairs that make up human DNA, store this information, improve data analysis tools, transfer the technology to the private sector for applied research, and address the related ethical, legal and social issues.

The goal of those who work in the field of genomic medicine is to integrate genomics into health applications. And while this field will play an increasingly important role in the diagnosis, monitoring and treatment of many diseases, many of the benefits are still years away.

Using genomics, researchers have been able to identify genetic defects which can either cause a disease or increase the susceptibility of contracting a disease. And with recent knowledge of how genes play a role in causing a disease, research can be focused on developing new therapies. Gene therapy may also be used to treat or potentially cure genetic and acquired diseases by replacing defective genes with normal genes. However, most human clinical trials of gene therapy are still in the research stages. Genetic counselors can only provide information and support (such as outlining options and helping to reduce risk among affected family members) to families who have members with birth defects or genetic disorders.

Pharmacogenomics is the convergence of pharmaceuticals and genetics. While still in the research phase, this field promises to provide drugs that can be adapted and customized for each individual based on their specific genetic makeup. This can lead to more powerful therapies, safer drugs with fewer side-effects, improved vaccines and the potential for improvements in the drug research and approval process.

There are many ethical, legal and social issues around genetic research. For example:

- Who owns your genetic information?
- Who will have access to it?
- Where will it be stored?
- Can an insurer refuse coverage given that a genetic condition increases the likelihood of contracting a disease?
- What would be the psychological impact on individuals who determine they have a propensity for contracting a disease?
- What would be is the impact if it is determined that a particular race or minority group is more likely to contract a disease?

Patenting DNA

As of the end of 2000, there were more than 25,000 DNA-based patents registered world-wide. In 2001, the U.S. Patent and Trademark Office published guidelines describing when gene sequences can be patented, in response to the raging debates around whether or not humans have the right to trademark genetic sequences.

According to the Patent Office's ruling, a genetic sequence can be patented by an organization if they disclose "how to use the purified gene isolated from its natural state". This means that if the organization can provide information as to a use for the gene, and can prove that they have cloned the gene themselves in a laboratory, then the genetic sequence can be considered their product.

Opponents of this type of patenting argue that following such logic, a person who carries a patented gene in their body could then be found guilty of patent infringement. They believe that a gene, as a naturally existing composition in nature, is not a product and thus shouldn't be patented. However, the U.S. Patent Office has a precedent for patenting natural products: in 1873 the Office granted Louis Pasteur a patent for yeast; adrenaline, too, when it was first discovered, was also patented.

Do you believe that organizations, academic or commercial, should have the right to patent the genetic sequences found in their research?

Portable Technology

Smart Card Technology in Medicine

A smart card is similar to a credit or debit card. However, instead of just a magnetic strip, it also contains data storage and a microprocessor. It is often used in a security application (for example, to gain access to secure areas or parking garages). A key difference between a credit/debit card and the smart card is the ability to change the stored information on the card. A cash card is a form of smart card. Some ATM machines have the ability to transfer cash from your bank account to the smart card, enabling you to purchase products and services from businesses that have the technology to extract cash for payment from your card. Examples of smart card include vending machines, automated toll booths on expressways and Internet access at Internet cafes.

Medical information can be stored on a smart card, giving health care institutions the ability to read your personal information digitally, rather than make you sit in an emergency triage center answering questions and filling out forms. This can result in lower administrative costs, faster diagnosis and treatment, and a higher degree of patient safety, because information regarding your past medical history, blood type, allergies and existing conditions would be readily available to emergency staff.

Issues and Challenges

There are many challenges to widespread adoption of smart cards for medical applications. The lack of standards among the many independent health-care organizations means that most smart card use is either within a single health organization or, potentially, in any country with socialized medicine. In this type of structure, it is possible to introduce mandatory standards and establish a system where an individual can access care at any of the health care offices or medical centers.

One of the main benefits of smart cards is the fact that they do not need to be connected to a central computer or network - all of the required information is stored on the card.

However, card loss or theft can be a serious problem unless there is a replication (or back-up) of the data contained on the card in a central system. As well, smart cards that have been updated at a physician's office without being connected to a central system will now contain different data. Without synchronization between the data stored centrally and on the card, the patient information could very quickly become out of date.

Fig. 2.1 A smart medical health card.

Embedded Devices

Similar to smart cards, these devices are embedded into the patient's body. They are about the size of a grain of rice. This technology is widespread in veterinary medicine as a way to identify animals. If you happen to lose a pet and it is returned to a shelter, a quick scan can determine whether a device is present. If so, the owner can easily be identified and the pet returned to its family. It is almost impossible to remove this device and it is tamper-resistant.

Embedded devices have the potential for many applications both in security and in medicine. They can also be combined with GPS technology to track an individual's movement. However, ethical, legal and social issues may prevent widespread adoption of these devices.

There are privacy concerns - for instance, what information is stored on the card? How is the information used? In the case of embedded chips, where the information is read wirelessly, how can the owner of a chip know when their information is being scanned?

Credit and debit card transactions are already tracked, leaving an electronic trail of information. The use of a smart card for payments or other transactions will also leave a digital trail.

Hand-held Computers and Wireless Technology

Hand-held technology, in the form of personal digital assistants (PDAs), is currently being used in hospitals for the delivery of patient information right to the bedside. This eliminates paper records and makes more information available to the physician at the time of need. Information available to hand-held computers can include images (e.g., MRI), test results, patient background, medications, allergies and records of pre-existing conditions. Images can be made simultaneously available to two physicians in different locations for consultations. In emergencies, a physician can be in another building and still have access to detailed and current information about the patient, if the hand-held computer is connected to a wireless network.

Medical Imaging

Medical imaging devices specialize in capturing images of various components of the human body. Early imaging included still images of internal structures (e.g., X rays). Current technology allows health-care professionals to view accurate three-dimensional images of moving tissue (e.g., a beating heart).

Magnetic Resonance Imaging

Magnetic Resonance Imaging (MRI) is used to create computer-generated three-dimensional renderings of internal body structures. While magnetic imaging has been in use for decades, it has evolved into a wide array of technologies and products. In the U.S. alone, it has grown into a $6 billion industry employing over 33,000 people.

The technology continues to evolve at a rapid pace, with much of the current research focused on adapting MRI technology to different areas of specialization and the specialized diagnosis of different diseases.

MRI is suited to diagnosing conditions and disorders affecting the central nervous system, bone structures, abdominal organs and blood vessels. New applications of the technology are under research.

Imaging Test for Diagnosing Breast Cancer

Researchers at the Mayo Clinic in Rochester, Minnesota, have developed an imaging technique using a combination of magnetic resonance imaging and sound waves. The procedure analyzes the properties of tissues within the breast and produces corresponding images. Since malignant tumors are typically much denser than breast tissue and benign tumors, this test is promising to identify malignant tumors with a high degree of accuracy. MRI alone yielded a high number of false positives (where a positive test result was incorrect). The goal of the research is to improve reliability and ultimately reduce the number of biopsies needed.

3-D Images of a Beating Heart

Cardiologists at Duke University Medical Center have estimated that about 30per cent of heart patients do not receive enough information from conventional imaging to determine an appropriate treatment. They developed the first MRI scanner in the U.S. that is dedicated solely to heart imaging. By capturing more detailed and accurate images, these researchers are able to differentiate between dead and damaged heart muscle tissue. As a result, a patient with damaged heart tissue can undergo a procedure (angioplasty or bypass surgery) to properly restore heart function.

Computed Axial Tomography

Computed Axial Tomography (CAT) scan uses a process of sending X rays through the body at various angles, resulting in cross-sectional images which are then combined using a computer to produce a three-dimensional image. While X rays are limited to certain structures (e.g., bones), a CAT scan can produce images of soft tissue, including organs. To make some organs and structures more visible under a CAT scan, a contrasting dye can be injected.

Ultrasound Imaging

Ultrasound (or sonography), the imaging of internal organs using high-frequency sound waves, has been in use in medicine since the Second World War. Recently, 3-D-rendering technologies (like those used in CAT scanning) have been combined with the two-dimensional imaging of ultrasound to create highly realistic and accurate three-dimensional images of the internal organs or structures being examined.

In obstetrics and gynecology especially, 3-D ultrasounds are growing more popular. Not only for the accuracy with which they allow doctors to diagnose health issues for the baby, but also with the parents - the 3-D ultrasound paints an almost exact image of what their baby looks like!

Positron Emission Tomography

Positron Emission Tomography (PET) is used to examine the human body at a molecular level. It can be used to measure brain activity and detect various brain disorders. It is one of the most effective technologies for the detection of certain types of cancers, including melanoma, lung, breast, colon, rectal and prostate cancer. It can not only identify tumors, but can determine whether they are malignant. PET can also assess heart muscle damage and detect restricted blood flow.

Medical Advice and Databases

Many new Web resources specializing in medicine have appeared in the past few years. An Internet search for the term "medical resources" using the Google search facility returns over 2.5 million links. While many of these are of limited value, the volume of information on the Web is staggering. Web portals or communities have emerged which are dedicated to provide a wide variety of resources, information and search tools to individuals and organizations with similar interests.

There are two groups of medical Web portals - those designed for health-care professionals and those for consumers.

Health Care Professionals

For health-care professionals, vast resources of medical information for virtually every specialty are available at a variety of medical Web portals or communities. These sites contain the latest research, access to discussion groups, reference material, news, events and anything else that may be of interest to each area of specialty. Physicians can search extensive medical databases, communicate with colleagues, explore new techniques and access professional development programs for Continuing Medical Education credit. The concept of Web communities is not new - associations for physicians and specialists, universities, libraries, government organizations and others have long had resources available to health-care professionals. What is new is the ease of access and world-wide availability enabled by the Internet and Web search technologies. With various search tools, the ability to get the material and other resources when you need them has been greatly enhanced.

Fig. 2.2 Medscape, a Web site for medical professionals.

Consumers

One of the leading medical Web portals designed for consumers is WebMD. This community provides a wealth of resources and includes tools to assess your symptoms, information on a wide variety of diseases and conditions, health and wellness resources, drug alerts and recalls, a complete medical library and even parenting and pregnancy information. It is a complete health information site with access to experts and live Webcast events. Medical information has been available for years, but typically in book or journal form available only through bookstores and libraries. Access to this information was a slow and tedious process. The very nature of the Internet has been a key enabling technology resulting in the development of Web portals like WebMD. Extensive medical information on virtually any medical subject is available with a few clicks. And with available search tools, access to information is faster and much more targeted to each user's specific needs.

As a by-product of this access, the consumer is becoming much more knowledgeable regarding health and medicine issues. Whether this knowledge translates into a healthier population and a lower cost per capita for health care, remains to be seen.

Fig. 2.3 webMD, medical resources for consumers.

Self-diagnosis via the Web

Have you used a Web-based medical site to look up symptoms, diseases or injuries? Many experts argue that having such specialized data available to people unschooled in properly interpreting it causes more harm than good. The first danger is erroneous self-diagnosis, where a patient decides on their own what their health problem is, and makes their own decisions on how to treat themselves. This problem can result in patients either taking over-the-counter drugs or medicine they don't need, or worse, concluding that their illness isn't as severe as it actually is and avoiding the proper medical care they need.

The other issue is ensuring the validity of the medical knowledge. Reliable portals such as WebMD aside, there are many other sources of medical information online, whose sources are not as easily verified. These could be Web sites of private businesses that present only the data that support their products, to personal Web sites publishing the author's opinion on a medical subject - neither of which is sufficient material on which to establish a diagnosis.

Do you think that free, unfettered access to medical information is better or worse for the patient?

Telemedicine

Telemedicine uses communications technology to deliver medical services to individuals in remote locations. It is used for a wide range of applications including diagnosis, care delivery, the transfer of patient data, consultation and education of health-care professionals. X rays, CT scans and MRI images can be transferred electronically between health care professionals for diagnosis. Many physicians have tools in their homes to receive information about patients, and to make decisions without the need to race to the hospital in urgent situations, saving time and reducing stress. Most of these situations used a store-and-forward process in which information is captured digitally, stored, and delivered electronically. Recent advances in information and communication technology allow real-time remote diagnostics. This can also include video transmissions, allowing the doctor to view the patient (and potentially the patient to see the doctor), or telemonitoring. Telemonitoring is the real-time monitoring of the patient's biological signals at a central care facility.

The National Aeronautics and Space Administration (NASA) played a major role in the early development and implementation of telemedicine. Sensors in both spacecraft and space suits were used to monitor the astronauts' various physiological parameters at lift-off, in space and on re-entry.

Emergency response teams use telemedicine to communicate with hospital staff to treat accident victims at the scene. Starting with simple voice communications, this application of telemedicine has evolved to the use of remote diagnostic tools to allow the emergency physician to immediately view the vital signs of a patient at the accident scene, and to direct treatment to stabilize the patient prior to transportation to the hospital.

Correctional facilities use telemedicine programs to reduce the cost and risk of transporting prisoners to health-care facilities.

Digital video transmissions can be used to allow physicians to see the patient and to establish a substitute for face-to-face contact.

There are many factors driving the implementation of telemedicine. Telemedicine has great potential to reduce health-care costs for rural and remote locations, as well as enhance the level of service to those outside major urban centers. Regional health centers can't possibly afford the technology and range of services available in larger cities. However, using telemedicine tools, patients located in small towns, on ships or even on an aircraft, can be connected, to specialists at a base unit located in a central facility by means of sensors attached to a mobile unit, that facilitates the transmission of real-time data., These specialists can be located anywhere in the U.S. (or in the world). This increases the range of services available to the rural population and optimizes the utilization of high-cost equipment and procedures at major health-care facilities.

Telesurgery

On September 7, 2001, Professor Jacques Marescaux and a 40-person team from the Institute for Research into Cancer of the Digestive System (IRCAD) performed the world's first telesurgery. From his facility in New York,Marescaux removed the gall bladder from a 68-year-old woman in Strasbourg, France. There were no complications and the patient returned home two days later.

The New York team used a video screen and controllers connected with high-speed fiber-optic line, and directed the arms of a surgical robot in an operating room at the European Institute of Telesurgery in Strasbourg. The operation lasted just under an hour.

The optimized compression technology developed by France Telecom was required to speed up video coding and decoding. This was combined with high-speed signal transmission to ensure that delays were minimized. A laparoscopic robot and software were developed specially for the project.

The total cost of the surgery was $1 million.

Challenges Faced by Telemedicine

Despite recent successes, there are many challenges to the adoption of telemedicine in the United States. First are privacy concerns: many worry about how the data will be used, and who really owns the data. Can hospitals record and sell medical monitoring data if the name of the patient is removed? Or does such data always belong to the patient? Then, there's the aspect of data security - what might happen if someone maliciously intercepts medical data and identifies it with a particular person?

The next challenge is bureaucratic: how to get around state licensing? Many states will not allow out-of-state physicians to practice in that state. In the case of telemedicine, where a medical expert might not even be located in the country, how does such licensing apply?

Medical insurers, too, have expressed reservations. Many private insurers will not reimburse for telemedicine consultations. Also, there is the question of liability - in the case of a problem, can the remote surgeon be charged with malpractice, even if complications may have been due to technical problems like robotic failure or loss of connection?

Finally, there is the financial bottom line. In cases of telemedicine where the patient is located in a different state from the medical doctor, how are the costs of equipment and communications shared between federal, state, and local health care? Moreover, the technology and network bandwidth available for telemedicine is simply not available in many rural or remote areas, even if it is a more cost-effective solution for them.

Indiana Heart Hospital

One of the major trends in health care is the move towards more specialization. This is being driven by the need to reduce costs. By specializing, hospitals can develop more scale and also develop efficiencies and expertise by narrowing their focus.

According to the National Center for Heath Statistics, heart disease is the leading cause of death in the U.S. with over 710,000 deaths occurring annually.

Opening in February 2003, the Indiana Heart Hospital is a state-of-the-art facility that was designed specifically to treat patients with heart disease. In designing the hospital for the future, 25per cent of the $60 million cost to build the hospital was invested in information systems and technology.

There are no nursing stations or record storage rooms. Hospital designers have implemented a paperless, filmless and wireless facility designed to reduce administrative costs and improve patient safety. There are an estimated 44,000 to 98,000 lives lost each year in the United States due to medical errors. Many of these are related to the use of paper-based systems and the unavailability of timely information. Digital technologies have the potential to reduce this number by up to 85per cent, according to the President of GE Medical, the hospital's technology partner.

The 88-bed hospital has almost 800 workstations - nine computers for each bed. There are no paper documents created at the hospital and all imaging is digital. All systems are seamlessly integrated to manage all of the processes, from admissions to release and billing.

Benefits include:

- reduced administrative costs
- faster patient processing and earlier treatment
- drug interaction monitoring
- immediate availability of detailed patient data - where and when required
- a reduction in errors
- improved patient safety

Technology and Disabilities

Influenced by the Americans with Disabilities Act (ADA), a wide range of products has emerged to support the use of computers by those who have various disabilities, including learning disabilities, visual impairment, deafness or limited motor functions. Section 508 of the Rehabilitation Act, which was amended in 1998, requires federal agencies to make technology accessible to those with disabilities. This includes computer hardware, software and related products such astraining material and Web sites).

For those that are visually impaired, there are braille keyboards and printers, large monitors and software which allows those with limited vision to enlarge the screen by "zooming in". Software is available to convert text to audio and to read documents aloud. Voice-recognition technology can be used to input text or dictate, and to issue voice commands to operate software. Web pages and documents like training manuals must be designed to provide descriptions of graphics and software navigation that provides keyboard alternatives to menu commands

Artificial Intelligence in Medicine

Artificial Intelligence (AI) is the science and engineering of attempting to create intelligent computers and software. AI specialists have made some progress in the creation of programs that display certain characteristics of human intelligence. Characteristics indicating intelligence include the ability to:

- acquire and use knowledge
- adapt to a changing environment
- communicate information
- reason
- develop strategies

Alan Turing (a British computer scientist, generally considered one of the fathers of artificial intelligence) maintained that a computer is intelligent if unbiased judges cannot tell the difference between computer-generated and human-generated output. By this simple definition (called the Turing Test), many computers and programs today could be considered intelligent, depending on the complexity of the task.

A program called ELIZA was developed by Joseph Weizenbaum in the 1960s. This program was designed to simulate a human therapist. As the user typed in comments or questions, the system responded with what appeared to be a normal response (at least, one that would seem normal coming from a therapist). In fact, the program created responses that re-used key words from the users' comments and questions in a context that seemed logical. For example, if you referred to your wife, the system would respond with "Tell me more about your wife".

In 1990, Hugh Loebner and the Cambridge Center for Behavioral Studies instituted the Loebner Prize, which awards $2,000 each year for the computer determined to be "most human". Human judges determine which computer's responses are the most indistinguishable from a human response.

Artificial intelligence has progressed significantly and computer power has grown exponentially, but AI has been applied to simpler tasks than originally contemplated. As technology continues to evolve and AI techniques become more sophisticated, there will no doubt be more "intelligent" computers performing more complex tasks in the future.

Applications of AI

Natural Language

The ability of computers to understand natural language - the human spoken language - is still limited. While computers can translate the spoken word into text (voice recognition) by simply translating each word in sequence, they have yet to develop the ability to interpret the meaning behind natural language. This is one of the difficulties with machine translation - the automatic translation between human languages. Many attempts have been made to invent computers that automatically translate text or speech between languages. While advancement has been made in this area, the human language has proven too complex for current technology and applications. The following is an example of text which has been translated from English into Spanish and back into English, using a popular machine-based translation service.

```
Telemedicine has the potential to reduce health care costs for rural
and remote locations, as well as enhancing the level of service to
those outside of major urban centers.

The telemedicina has the potential to reduce the medical costs of aid
for remote and rural locations, as well as also enlarging the level of
the service to those greater urban outside of centers.
```

As you can see, this type of translation can provide the basic meaning with some interpretation, but for critical applications this would not be acceptable. The software had difficulty with the term telemedicine. It also had difficulty with the subtle difference in meaning between enhance and enlarge and with the syntax of the last part of the sentence. It is expected that within five to ten years, machine translation will have evolved to a point where it is a practical, low-cost alternative to human translation, with little appreciable difference in the quality.

Expert Systems

These are computer systems that use rules developed by experts in a certain field and apply these rules, together with information stored in a knowledge base, to draw the same conclusions as the expert would.

Neural Networks

Neural networks are designed to simulate the structure of the human brain. Just as the human brain contains billions of interconnected neurons, neural networks interconnect thousands of processors in multiple ways.

AI and Diagnosis

A study in late 1997 at the University Hospital in Lund, Sweden, compared the interpretation of electrocardiograms (ECGs) by experienced cardiologists and by computer-based technology using artificial neural networks. The neural networks were found to be 10 per cent more accurate than the most experienced cardiologists. Considering that 25 per cent of ECG readings are misinterpreted, this technique shows some promise in potentially saving lives. The AI technique used in this case will not replace the cardiologist's interpretation, as the cardiologist also considers other factors not assessed by the neural network (e.g., the patient's mood). However, in the hands of an experienced cardiologist, this could be a very valuable tool in increasing diagnostic accuracy.

AI and Testing for Cervical Cancer

Among all cancers, cervical cancer is second only to breast cancer as a leading cause of death among women. As with all cancer, early diagnosis is critical to effective treatment. Screening of pap smear specimens is the traditional diagnostic tool for detecting the presence of cervical cancer cells. The accuracy of manually-screened pap smears is limited, which potentially places women at risk. A false positive result will lead the patient to believe she has cancer when in fact she doesn't. This will certainly cause anxiety, but she will eventually get good news. A false negative, on the other hand, can cause serious consequences. A woman with cervical cancer can go for months without being diagnosed correctly and the delay in treatment can have serious or potentially fatal consequences.

Using a combination of Artificial Neural Networks (ANN) and image processing technology, automated screening can be performed with a high degree of accuracy. Three automated pap screening methods have received FDA approval. According to the FDA, when used with a manual screening process, these systems will "considerably decrease the likelihood of missing the diagnosis of cervical cancer".

Faster and more scalable diagnosis can result in earlier detection, an increased rate of success for treatment, reduced costs for care and treatment, and ultimately, a healthier population.

New Blood Test for Cancer Diagnosis

In a joint program between the FDA and the National Cancer Institute, scientists have used artificial intelligence techniques to develop a blood test which can detect various types of cancer with an accuracy of 90per cent or higher. A single drop of blood is all that is needed. Tests have already been conducted on breast, ovary and lung cancer tissue. The scientists involved in the research believe that the test can be applied to other forms of cancer too.

The Artificial Nose

Electronic artificial noses are being developed for use in medical, environmental and industrial applications. Using artificial neural network technology and a chemical sensing system, the nose can detect odors resulting from infection, glucose levels in diabetics and conditions such as tuberculosis.

In many cases, technological advances have resulted in diagnostic technologies that are more accurate than expert physicians. Will this form of diagnosis ultimately replace physicians? Or will human intervention always be needed, and artificial intelligence remain simply another tool in the physician's bag?

Lifetime Medical Records

According to the British Institute of Medicine, when a patient visits his/her physician, 70 per cent of the physician's needs for information are not met.

The British government plans to spend £5.2 million on information systems to connect all health care facilities and develop standards for sharable health records. The program will provide physician practices with a 256-Kbps connection to the main network, and larger facilities with a 2-Mbps fixed-link connection. All Britons will use their National Health Service number as the key to accessing services anywhere in the country. A master patient index is being built, which, when complete, will provide physicians anywhere in the country with the relevant information on each patient. All vendors participating in the project must conform to strict standards for electronic health records, to ensure compatibility. The first phase is expected to be complete in 2005, with full implementation by 2008. The benefits of the program include more convenient access to facilities, faster admission, lower administrative costs and the introduction of new services, such as on-line booking of appointments.

Given that Britain has a socialized or public health care system and the U.S. has a private system, is this type of initiative possible in the United States? What are the barriers? What about insurance providers, health maintenance organizations (HMOs), etc.?

3

COMPUTER TECHNOLOGY in
Arts & Entertainment

Overview

Traditionally, the tools used to create a particular work of art have rigidly defined the creative process. For instance, to create a painting, the canvas first was to be prepared a certain way, then the sketch was drawn on the canvas, then the artist added the oil colors to make the final painting. Many considered it impossible to deviate from this order and still produce a quality work of art.

The computer has helped change this type of thinking, liberating the artist in two main ways:

- The creative tools no longer define the creative process
- The creative process is not as strongly limited by chronological restrictions

To illustrate the first point, consider the following: The same artist creating the painting above in computer software could draw a rough sketch using colors, thus defining the palette for the piece. Then she could create a more detailed sketch, apply the colors and even some of the color shapes drawn previously to those details. Then the whole painting is printed in color on paper, which is used as a model for the oil painting the artist will paint by hand on canvas. The end result is still an oil painting, but with a drastically different creative process.

To explain the second point, consider this: with a computer, the artist is free to start and stop the creative process with far fewer restrictions. Paint might dry, musicians might fall asleep, actors need to be paid overtime, but the computer is ready any time inspiration strikes.

The arts affected by computers are not only painting, but of course every discipline that has any connection to the arts, no matter how tenuous. This chapter will examine the computer's effect on music in detail, then briefly examine influences on graphic arts, television, film, and live performance arts.

Music

Probably the single most important development computer technology has brought to music has been to enable computer software to perform tasks that were normally the sole responsibility of very expensive hardware in very expensive music studios. At present, even a modest computer combined with well-made music software and a minimum of musical hardware (such as a high quality sound card and a microphone) allows any musician to compose, record, mix, and master studio-quality music, all from the same computer.

Bear in mind that, even though using a computer to help create music might simplify some of the tasks a musician faces and might allow that musician to accomplish more with fewer resources, it is not a substitute for musical talent.

Overview

There are four main formats for creating music with a computer: MIDI, synthesis, sampling, and audio. Almost all computer music software will combine most, if not all, of these formats.

MIDI

Musical Instrument Digital Interface is a technology developed in the early 1980s by synthesizer manufacturers to enable instruments made by different companies to be used together.

MIDI is a communications protocol for controller synthesizers and other musical instruments. Think of MIDI as similar to notes written on sheet music. The notes on the staff give the musician instructions such as which notes to play, when each note should be played, and how long each note should be. The sheet music also suggests how loud to play each note, how fast the song should be played, and which instruments should play which part.

MIDI performs exactly the same function. MIDI commands (called "events") are sent digitally to a synthesizer (or a virtual instrument on a computer) which then translates them into sounds. This is how you can use the same electronic keyboard to play any synthesizer or digital instrument - the only information being sent is that which describes how the music is to be played. No actual audio is being sent at all.

Because MIDI is simply a series of binary numbers, it can be recorded to software, played back and edited, just like any other computer file. Software that performs these tasks is known as a "sequencer".

Originally, piano-style keyboards were the first instruments to be used as MIDI controllers, and are the most commonly found MIDI controller today. However, models based on other traditional instruments also exist. There are MIDI drum kits, MIDI guitars, MIDI wind instruments (a reed instrument similar to the saxophone or the clarinet), and even MIDI valve instruments (like the trumpet). Any of these instruments can be connected to software or hardware to allow the musician to play it in the same way they would play the real instrument.

General MIDI

Like any computer protocol being developed simultaneously by more than one manufacturer, the first implementations of MIDI had inconsistencies from one manufacturer's product to the next. For instance, the message that played a middle C on one synthesizer might play a low C on another. Or perhaps the sound setting marked "piano" on one instrument might correspond on another not to a piano, but to a tuba! The reason behind this is that events like MIDI notes or changing the instrument ("program changes") are simply numbers, ranging from 000-127. At the time, each manufacturer was free to assign these numbers arbitrarily for their own products, as they saw fit.

In 1991, the MIDI Manufacturer's Association established a standard called General MIDI. This standard lays out the specifications for MIDI messages (like assigning note numbers, initiating program changes, etc.) in order to eliminate situations like those described above. If a piece of software or an instrument has been branded as GM compatible, this means that it will sound the same when played by or with any other GM-compatible hardware or software.

Synthesis

Technically, sound synthesis came before MIDI. As early as the 1940s, scientists across the world experimented with creating instruments that produce sound electronically - not to be confused with electro-mechanical instruments like the organ, which produces sound the usual mechanical way (percussion, vibrating strings, etc.) and which augments the sound with electronics. The synthesizer, instead, uses electronics to produce a sound wave, and then shapes that wave in ways that are more musically pleasing. Analog synthesizers (where the sounds are produced by electronics) became fashionable in popular music during the 1960s and 1970s, and digital synthesizers (in which the sounds are produced and modified by microchips) followed close behind during the 1980s.

Computer software can digitally produce the same types of synthesis as its hardware counterparts, and even more of them. While the first software versions of synthesizers tried to recreate sounds from "vintage" synthesizers of the 60s, 70s, and 80s, many more are being created that have an original sound entirely their own.

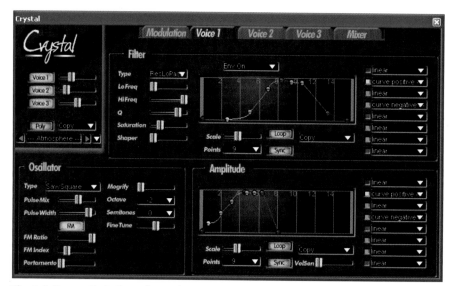

Fig. 3.1 Green Oak Crystal: a software synthesizer famous for its unique sound.

Sampling

Back in the late 1970s, the problem with synthesizers was that, even though they were good at creating new and unique sounds, they couldn't convincingly replicate the sound of "real" instruments. Enter the sampler: an electronic device which plays a very short recording of a real instrument (say, one note from a piano) instead of trying to generate its own sound to emulate a piano. The recording of the note is then pitched up or down (played faster or slower) to make up the various pitches of the musical scale.

Hardware samplers in the 1980s became much more powerful than simply playing single notes pitched higher or lower. Entire bars of music could be recorded and played back in an endless loop, or different sections of a drum beat could be remixed (the sampler was one of the hallmarks of rap and hip hop music during that decade, and still remains so today). However, the amount of recorded audio the hardware sampler could keep in its memory was very limited. The software sampler on a computer, with hard drives that can hold hundreds of gigabytes of music, is not constrained by this limitation. Add to that digital signal processing (DSP) and easy-to-manipulate graphical interfaces (hardware samplers were restricted to a few buttons and a small LED screen), and the computer took the sampler to a whole new level.

Digital Audio

As you might remember from physics class, sound is really just waves vibrating through a surface (like air). Magnetic audio tape records a representation of the wave directly to tape, which is then translated back into an audio signal by the tape recorder when played. This is called analog audio.

That wave can be plotted on a graph, with values generally from -1.0 to 1.0. Digital audio records a signal by slicing up the wave into tiny sections (called samples) and then records the slice's value for that particular slice, each value representing a single point on the graph. Compact discs, the most successful mass market implementation of digital audio, use a sample rate of 44,100 Hz. That means that when CD-quality audio is captured digitally, the wave's value is recorded 44,100 times in one second.

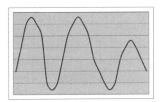
An analog wave: continuous movement

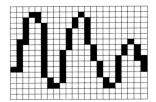
The digital signal: blocky, because it only records the shape of the wave at every sample.

Fig. 3.2 Analog vs. digital waves

However, CD-quality audio recording is nothing new, having been in use since the early 1980s. So how have computers now advanced the capabilities of audio recording?

- Disk storage space.
  Larger, faster hard drives allow for real-time recording of hours and hours of audio.

- Higher quality digital-to-analog converters.
  44,100 Hz sampling for digital audio is good, but it's still not perfect, and does not recreate a sound anywhere near as accurately as the human ear can interpret it. Digital-audio converters (DACs), the hardware that converts the signal to binary for the computer to understand (and back again) are available today that can sample the signal as fast as 192,000 Hz. The size of the data in each sample (called "bandwidth" or "bit-depth") is higher, too. CD-quality sound has a bit depth of 16 bits per sample. The latest DACs are capable of 24 bits per sample. The more bits per sample, the finer the volume range the DAC can produce.

- Intuitive software for digital audio editing.
  Keyboards and samplers from the 1980s were known for their tiny LCD screens that were difficult to read and even harder to navigate through. With an entire computer screen to show as much detail as the user could want, and the now-intuitive actions of point, click, drag and drop with the mouse, software offers the user much more visual feedback and control than hardware.

Software

Like musical instruments and hardware, there are several main types of music software.

Old-school: the 4-track recorder

Most computer music and audio software is modelled on the old 4-track tape recorder. Instead of simply playing back two channels of audio (stereo: right and left), the 4-track recorder allows you to record each of 4 channels separately, and then mix them together as you need to. The big advantage of the 4-track recorder is that any or all channels can be played back while the rest are recording. Thus, an entire song can be created as each part is layered one on top of the other.

For instance, a capable musician could, say, record a bass line for an entire song on the first track. Then, while the bass line is playing back, the same musician would record the acoustic guitar part for the song. The musician then plays those two tracks and records a drum part on the third track. Finally, with all three tracks playing, the musician records the vocals onto track four. This type of layering, known as multi-tracking, is the basis for most computer music software.

Sequencers

The first sequencers for computer were MIDI-only versions of the multi-track recorder. Since then, the term sequencer has really come to include all-in-one workstation software for editing and recording digital audio and MIDI together. Most sequencers also operate as hosts for at least one type of software plugin (see below), which is used to expand its musical capabilities.

Pro Tools

For many years now, Digidesign Pro Tools has been the de facto standard in digital audio sequencing in professional studios across the world. The key to Pro Tools has always been that a "Pro Tools rig" (as they are known) is not just the software sequencer, but also is made up of proprietary digital signal processing (DSP) cards for the computer to share the load of audio processing with the CPU, and often a control surface/mixing board too, to control the recording software by hand. Pro Tools are generally considered "high end" studio gear, and as such are usually found in professional studios.

Cubase SX

However, the biggest change computer technology brings to music is that it is possible for the amateur or semi-professional musician to make professional-quality recordings and music in a home studio. Steinberg Cubase SX is a sequencer that enables just such a revolution. Cubase SX can manipulate tracks of audio and MIDI together with ease, and coming from the company that invented the VST plugin (see below), has a full complement of effects and tools plugins for manipulating the sound.

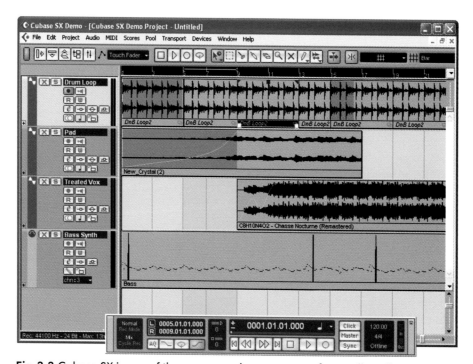

Fig. 3.3 Cubase SX is one of the more popular sequencers for small studios

Audio Editors

A sequencer is best-suited to layering tracks to create full songs. However, there are many times when a tool is needed that is better suited to more utilitarian tasks, such as trimming the excess sound off a short recording before it is sequenced into the song, or perhaps to assign loop points to a recording of an organ note before it is loaded into a sampler. For these tasks, the software known as an audio editor is best. While many sequencers do have some audio editing features, often it is best to have an audio editor around as well to take care of the more detailed edits that the sequencer can't handle.

Sound Forge

Sonic Foundry Sound Forge is one of the long-time favorite audio editors. In addition to standard audio editing tasks, Sound Forge can also apply DirectX effect plugins (another format of audio software plugin) to audio files, and process batches of separate audio files.

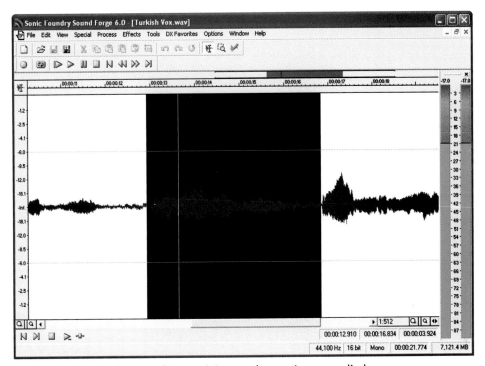

Fig. 3.4 Sonic Foundry Sound Forge 6.0 at work, creating an audio loop.

Software Instruments

In addition to functioning as a multi-track studio recorder, there are also complete musical instruments in stand-alone software format (stand-alone as opposed to plugins - see below). Almost all of these instruments rely on receiving MIDI input to be controlled by the musician, though some have keyboard/mouse input, and a few might even accept other forms of input.

Most instrument software is designed to be a synthesizer of some sort, or to emulate a vintage instrument. However, some software, such as Ableton Live, blurs the definition of classifications like sequencer or instrument. Billing itself as a "sequencing instrument", Live plays music loops (drum beats, synth lines, guitar riffs, etc.), automatically synchronizing them to the chosen tempo. The musician triggers the loops in whichever way s/he wants, and can apply special effects to the results in realtime, thus remixing the music in an improvisational way.

Hardware

Experts will argue endlessly about the sound quality of this piece of expensive studio hardware versus that piece of expensive studio hardware. Real or imagined audiophile differences aside, currently the technology has come to a point where there are really only three pieces of hardware needed to create music: a computer, a sound card, and a MIDI controller. Two more pieces of equipment are needed if the musician wants to record acoustic music: a microphone and a mixer (or pre-amplifier) to plug it into.

Computer Essentials

Computer music software has been around since the days of the Commodore 64. However, to tap the full potential of most modern music software, you should probably have at least a Pentium III (for Windows or Linux), or a G3 processor (for Macintosh). CPU speed and RAM are the key. The more, the better.

Sound Card

A sound card is essential for computer music - it is the way that audio and/or MIDI gets in and out of the computer. The higher quality the digital-analog converter on the sound cardsound card, the better the sound you will get from the computer. Sound cards that play audio at 192 kHz with a depth of 24-bits are miles above the bargain 16-bit 44.1 kHz sound cards that come installed with many computers.

Most sound cards exist that plug into the computer as an internal component. However, portable sound cards also exist in external format, often as USB or firewire interfaces. These external sound cards enable laptop computers to become carry out musical studio activities "on the go"

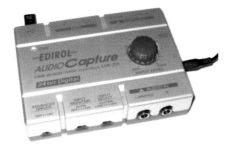

Fig. 3.5 Edirol UA-20: a 24-bit audio USB audio and MIDI interface ideal for laptop musicians

MIDI Controller

Many enterprising musicians get by with simply the computer, the software, and the sound card. However, any musician who requires hands-on control of an instrument would do well to get a MIDI controller, typically a keyboard.

Microphone and Mixer

The small microphone that comes with some computer sound cards might be enough for Internet phone applications, but for musical purposes, something a little more robust is needed. Many semi-professional quality microphones require power from a mixer, or at least require amplification (known as a "pre-amp") before the signal is recorded. This can be accomplished with a small mixer, or better yet, many higher-quality sound cards have what is called a "break-out box".

A break-out box is a separate attachment to the sound card which houses extra input and output ports, and often has hardware specifically for recording (like a microphone pre-amp).

The One-Man Band?

All this powerful music software means that one computer can now carry all the tools to enable its user to wear several different hats: song-writer, musician, singer, studio producer, and mastering engineer, to name simply a few.

Thanks to this new-found freedom, more and more musicians these days are going solo with their musical ventures, handling everything themselves and often just delivering a final copy of an album to their recording company to be pressed straight to CD. This is especially true in electronic music, where the songs are composed almost exclusively of parts generated and played by the computer.

But what effect does this have on music? How essential is the human element in performance and interpretation of music? Can a series of MIDI tracks be considered real music, even though the melodies were never actually played by a person, but were simply programmed by a mouse into a grid of notes? Even when a traditional composer writes a song, it is performed and interpreted by real musicians, often several.

And what effect might the lack of other musicians have on the music? Bob Moog, the inventor of the first commercially successful synthesizer in the 1970s, was asked in a recent interview in Wired magazine what his thoughts were on the future of electronic music. His reply: "I have concerns. A hundred years ago, music was a social thing - musicians would face one another and bond through sound. Now, everybody is by himself. I think of the Minimoog Voyager [synthesizer] as a thing you play with other people. I hope I'm increasing the social aspect of making music."

The "Complete" Music Studio

So, is it possible to have a truly complete music studio on a computer? Most professional music producers, while they do use computers in the studio, still insist that software can't do everything, and certain pieces of hardware (especially those for adding effects to the music, like reverb or compression) simply cannot be replaced.

However, for every possible purpose for which hardware electronics are used in making music, a piece of software has probably been developed to carry out that same task. In particular, the following software innovations are driving a movement to "do it all virtually".

Plugins

A plugin is a computer program that cannot be run on its own. Instead, it runs inside another program (known as a host). Web browsers, for example, use plugins to display content that they normally couldn't on their own (like Macromedia Flash). Plugins in music software add features that the software doesn't have, like a synthesizer instrumentor a reverb effect.

There are several major types of plugin format:

Virtual Studio Technology (VST) plugins

VST plugin technology was developed by the German software company Steinberg for their sequencer, Cubase, as an open standard for any developer to use to create their own plugins. The VST standard is cross-platform (PC and Macintosh) and is probably the most commonly-supported plugin format.

Direct-X plugins

Using technology from Microsoft's Direct-X audio/video standard, Direct-X plugins are another format that is gaining popularity. Direct-X plugins are available only for Windows-compatible software.

Audio Units

Audio Units are plugins developed specifically for the Macintosh OSX platform, to make use of its built-in Core Audio processing features. Audio Unit plugins are streamlined for performance on OSX, but are also restricted to that operating system.

RTAS

RTAS is the plugin format made by Pro Tools for its own software and hardware. While this means a rather restricted user base for this format, it is often still worthwhile for developers to create an RTAS version of a plugin because of the high number of commercial studios that have a Pro Tools rig.

All-in-one Software

Traditionally, using the computer to make music involves working with several different stand-alone applications in tandem. However, some computer music software attempts to do it all. These "all-in-one" software studios do have an advantage in that each piece is optimized to work well with the rest of the software. However, software studios are usually not extensible - that is, they cannot be expanded in any way (as with plugins).

Reason

Propellerhead Reason is one such software studio. Reason uses a hardware-like "rack" to hold all its components onscreen, making it more intuitive for musicians who might not be so comfortable with a computer. Reason has instruments (several types of synthesizer as well as a few types of sampler), effects (reverb, compressor, delay, distortion - all the essential classics), and even two types of sequencer for putting the music together.

Modular Audio Environments

Another form of musical software that is rapidly gaining popularity is that which uses a modular approach to building the sound. Instead of using the preset routing used by most software sequencers (such as track > mixer > effects send > mixer > output), it falls to the user to lay out the modules through which each channel of audio will flow.

By connecting modules and drawing the flow of the audio with the mouse, modular audio applications take full advantage of the visual control over software that computers allow.

Max/MSP

Cycling 74's Max/MSP for the Macintosh is probably one of the most well-known pieces of modular audio software. An especial favorite of abstract audio artists and experimental electronic musicians, Max/MSP's big attraction is that (with a bit of background in digital signal processing theory) the musician can design his or her own original DSP effects.

Plogue Bidule

A newcomer to the computer music scene, Plogue Bidule is an example of a popular new type of audio software: the modular VST host. In Bidule, users can load VST plugins, draw connections between them in any way they like, and add any number of Bidule's built-in modules for routing, mixing, and modifying MIDI and audio in any way imaginable. Modular hosts like this grant the musician maximum control over every aspect of the sound, at the cost of a little planning and preparation.

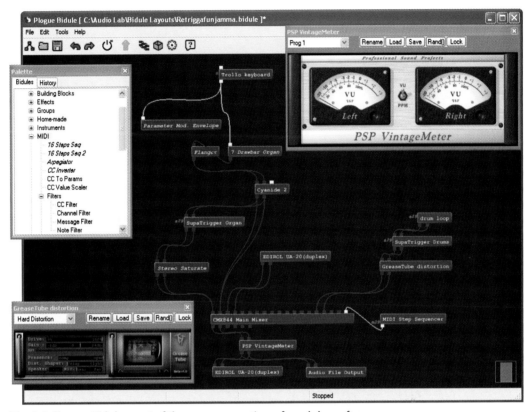

Fig. 3.6 Plogue Bidule, part of the new generation of modular software

Quantity over Quality?

Now that home computers have made quality music production software available to the masses, will that have a positive or a negative effect on new music?

One thing is obvious... the tools for producing music on the computer are making certain tasks much easier and more accessible to a greater number of people. This has meant an exponential increase in the number of what's known as "bedroom producers" - that is, musicians who record and make their music on computers at home. Add to that the many online Web sites where musicians can market and host their own music for little or no cost (like MP3.com or IUMA.com), and the reality is that anyone can easily publish whole albums of music without ever having to go through a recording company or the music publishing industry at all.

Some argue that this makes it easier for lesser-known musicians to make themselves familiar to audiences across the world and to gain their own foothold in the music market. Others argue that when the quality-control checks represented by recording companies are removed, it simply opens the floodgates to a glut of poorly-made music. What is your opinion on the subject?

Computer Music Online

Music software for the personal computer may have opened up professional production to the masses, but the global connection of the Internet is what has been the real boost behind this trend. Musicians can market their music on the World Wide Web, share knowledge and resources, as well as collaborate with other artists, no matter how far removed they are geographically.

Web Resources

Developer Web pages, software and hardware review sites, online forums, insider industry news sources, online sample libraries... there are hundreds of places online to find resources for making music on the computer, not including the thousands of personal Web pages devoted to self-published music.

Industry Forums

Nowhere does the Internet's idea of the global community shine through more than on the public forums. These are places where industry leaders as well as beginner musicians all meet to discuss music and production of music on the computer. These are good places to ask for advice, and find people who know the answers.

Internet Collaboration

In addition to asking for advice, having access to the Internet not only makes musical collaboration faster, but also makes it possible in parts of the world where it was simply impossible before.

RocketNetwork

The ability to trade files for a music project via e-mail or FTP is useful, certainly, but there are also services devoted specifically to creating collaboration between musicians. Pro Tools, for example, uses technology originally developed by a company called RocketNetwork (acquired in 2003 by Avid - the company that owns Pro Tools), to build collaboration features directly into the Pro Tools software. Users can connect to the RocketNetwork server over the Internet, and work in real-time on the same project - adding tracks, editing, deleting, etc.

Listening to Music on the Computer

Finally, the use of the computer as a music listening station should not be overlooked. Prior to the rise in popularity of the MP3 file, one might listen to a CD on the computer, but for the most part, when it came to entertainment, the computer was relegated to video games.

The M-peg Layer 3 audio file format changed all that. Songs could be copied from a CD to the computer, yet only take up one tenth of the disk space. The legal issues of Internet file-trading aside, MP3-sharing propelled the computer head-first into the realm of entertainment unit.

The Cost of Music File Sharing

Made popular with Napster in 1999, peer-to-peer (P2P) file sharing operates like this: one user takes a CD and copies all the songs on it to MP3 files on his/her computer. Then, through software like Napster, other users can access the music files on the first user's computer and copy them to their own. In turn, other users can access all the music files stored on any other user's computer connected to the same network.

Legally, the owner of a CD is allowed to make one copy for their own listening, but not to give away or share with anyone else. Especially not with hundreds and hundreds of anonymous users online. The music industry claim that P2P file sharing is costing them and the artists they represent millions of dollars in CD sales every year.

However, most of the people sharing music on P2P networks claim that it is the vastly inflated cost of CDs (of which the artist generally sees only a small fraction) that is driving them to download music. With music being so expensive, they argue, they need to "test" music out before buying it. In fact, there are just as many independent studies claiming that P2P music sharing actually helps music sales, as there are saying that it hurts them.

The biggest player in the fight against P2P file sharing is the Recording Industry Association of America (RIAA). They were the legal force behind shutting down P2P networks such as Napster, AudioGalaxy, and Morpheus. Recently, they have also targeted legal action against specific individuals identified as having made large quantities of music files available for others to download. In May 2003, the RIAA sued four university students (Aaron Sherman and Jesse Jordan of Rensselaer Polytechnic Institute, Daniel Peng of Princeton University, and Joseph Nievelt of Michigan Technological University) for $150,000 per copyrighted work that was downloaded.

Obviously, the suits were intended more to scare other P2P users than to actually try winning that much money from the four students. The four settled out of court for total amounts ranging from $12,000 to $17,500. Has the scare tactic worked? How prevalent is file sharing among people you know?

Music Formats for Computer

In addition to MP3, there are many other popular file formats for listening to music on the computer. MP3 and the open-source Ogg Vorbis are two cross-platform (available for PC, Macintosh, and Linux) methods of compressing audio data into a file size roughly one tenth of the original, uncompressed wave.

Speaking of uncompressed audio, the WAV file is the standard for storing pure digital audio on the PC and Linux, while the equivalent standard for Macintosh is the AIFF.

The Internet and Musical Distribution

Downloading complete files from the Internet to a computer is fine if the user has the time to wait, but something also needs to be done for those users who want to listen to real-time audio but who are impeded by slower Internet connections. The solution is to stream the file, which means downloading a little bit at a time, and playing that first bit while the rest of the file is still being downloaded. Real Audio was the first major format to gain popularity that way. With higher bandwidth on Internet connections, many other file formats can be streamed across the Internet, including MP3.

Online Music Sales

A new distribution style for music, interestingly enough, is based in part on file downloading networks like Napster. Apple's online iTunes Music Store, launched in May 2003, processed at least 200,000 song purchases and downloads on its opening day. The price tag: $0.99 per song. Listen.com's music file download-purchasing service, Rhapsody, lowered its download fee by $0.20 to $0.79 per song at the beginning of May (to compete with Apple, presumably). Numbers announced by the company in July indicate that music downloads for the service increased by 100% during June 2003.

Is this the new distribution model for buying music? It could be. At its launch, Apple's iTunes catalog consisted of only works licensed from the larger record companies, but Apple recently started marketing the network to small and independent record labels, promising equal coverage for their music, and pricing that was no better or worse than that offered by the larger labels.

If many of these independent record labels start using iTunes for distribution, what do you think the outcome will be? Will the downloadable file come to replace the CD entirely? Or is there still a place in the music industry for both formats?

Managing Works of Art

By entering the digital medium, art becomes a very different thing altogether. Much more easily copied, viewed and manipulated, art on the computer becomes subject to a whole new range of advantages and disadvantages for artist and audience alike.

Distribution & Licensing

Just as it did for music, the Internet has literally opened up a whole new world for the distribution and licensing of art of all kinds. Artists can sell their art online to reach markets all over the world.

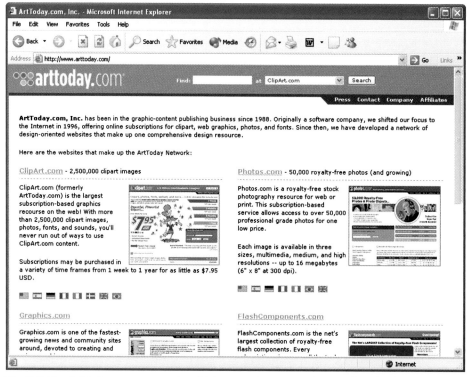

Fig. 3.7 The ArtToday.com network, which comprises several sites of art for licensing or royalty-free sales services, selling everything from clipart to digital photography, to Macromedia Flash objects for Web design.

Digital Rights Management

Digital rights management is a very big and hotly contested subject. Essentially, digital rights management is a system or technology for controlling the use and/or distribution of a digital file (usually music or video).

There are two main types of DRM: watermarking, which consists of marking the file content with a symbol (or a sound in the case of audio files) that makes the content impossible to reproduce in its watermarked form; and encryption, which somehow scrambles the content of the digital file so that it can only be properly viewed in an application or device specifically designed for decrypting it.

Windows "Longhorn" and the Next Generation Secure Computing Base

At the Windows Developers' Conference in 2003, Microsoft announced the latest incarnation of their operating system (currently code-named "Longhorn") and one of its core features, the Next Generation Secure Computing Database (NGSCB). Essentially, the NGSCB works hand-in-hand with optimized hardware, providing very powerful security and data encryption features. These encryption features could also conceivably be used for applying and enforcing digital rights management. While many uses of the NGSCB make sense for copy protection (enforcing software licenses, for instance), some privacy experts argue that these features could be used to keep certain software applications from opening certain files, or even to allow software to operate only on certain operating systems.

Sculpture

Sculpture, being a form of art that requires three-dimensional space, does not immediately strike one as an art form that would easily take to computer technology. However, many tools exist for just that purpose, and many artists are taking advantage of them. These tools enable sculptors to use the computer in two main ways: during the sculpture design process, where mock-ups and variations of the art can be modelled and planned out on the screen (CAD drawings are a good example of this type of application); and during the production process, where computers controlling specially designed machines can be used to cut the materials, or build the sculpture from scratch.

3-D Rendering as Sculpted Art

A sculpture is three-dimensional. A rendered 3-D image or CAD drawing contains three-dimensional information. Should this be considered any less a sculpture than if the artist created it using hammer and chisel instead of mouse and software?

Hands-on: Force Feedback Control

Haptics is the science of using computer-controlled force feedback to simulate touch. As an art that is traditionally all about hands-on control, sculpture is a perfect fit for haptics. Sculptors can use products like the FreeForm system by SensAble Technologies to "carve" 3-D images on-screen with a specialized tool. The FreeForm tool (shaped like a long pencil or stick) is connected to a device which relays pressure back to the tool, making the artist feel as though the tool is actually touching the 3-D object seen on the computer screen.

Computer Technology on the Stage

Even in live human performance arts like theatre and dance, computer technology is beginning to play a strong supporting role. Instead of replacing actors and human creativity, it is instead being used to enhance the technical side of the show - controlling the the lighting, the sound effects, and even sometimes visual effects and props via software.

Dance

Dance, being an art centered around the human body and its movements, has rarely involved computers for more than auxiliary support, such as automated control of stage and occasionally music (if the dancers are not accompanied by live musicians). However, two computer technologies have started to find a greater influence on modern dance: computer-assisted choreography, and telematics (the computer analysis of movement).

Computer-assisted Choreography

Like almost every other discipline, dancers are also starting to turn to the computer to help with administrative or mechanical tasks. There is a small but growing market for choreographical software; for instance, programs that help plan, record, or present choreography. Two popular applications are Laban Writer and Life Forms Dance.

Laban Writer is a software editor for recording choreography using the Laban Dance Notation language (originally developed by Rudolph Laban in the 1920s).

Life Forms Dance, by Credo Interactive, is a 3-D animation studio specializing in creating animations of dancer movement, specifically to choreograph dances. The software comes with a large library of pre-made poses and movements (including one designed specifically for classical ballet), and the choreographer can also create his or her own. Once choreographed, the software can play the animation as a video, a visual 3-D model for the dancers to learn from and follow.

Telematics

Telematics is the recording, analysis, and playback of movement on the computer. Using motion-capture technology, choreographers can record the movements of multiple points on a dancer's body simultaneously. With the 3-D rendering software, these movements can then be used in any creative way imaginable: to create virtual dancers, to add visual effects to a recording of the dance, to project an image of the dancer into a virtual space… the possibilities are only beginning to be explored. Telematics has also long been used in film for the creation of virtual characters or to add special effects to a living character. But now that computer technology has progressed to the point where many visual effects can be applied live, live artistic performance, like dance, is the logical new application.

Computer Technology in Film

The film industry long ago adopted the computer as an indispensable tool for producing films, in everything from the planning and paperwork to the development and application of the very latest in special effects and visual editing. In fact, many of the processes now commonly used in film were often developed out of need or necessity, when a producer needed to create a certain type of effect that was not yet possible. Popular films like Star Wars, Toy Story, or the Matrix are responsible for the genesis of many new and powerful technologies which have gone on to become staples in the film industry.

Film-making can be generalized into three stages: pre-production, production, and post-production. Some of the modern uses of computer technology in each area are examined below.

Pre-production

Pre-production can be classified as the planning stage of the film. This includes everything from project management, budgeting, storyboards of camera shots, and pre-visualization of potential scenes to be recorded.

Film-making Planning Software

Just like project management software for commercial business, there is also film planning and production management software for the film industry. CineMatrix Professional is one such application. It combines tools designed specifically for the directing, technical planning, and budgetary aspects of film project management with computing advantages such as file management or project data sharing with multiple users.

3-D Rendered Animations for Pre-visualization

With computer processing power increasing, and 3-D rendered animation becoming more commonplace, many directors have started to create 3-D rendered animations of tricky camera shots before the recordings are actually made. Shots that require blending many differently-sized components make this kind of "shot drafting" necessary, especially for movies like Star Wars: Episode II or Lord of the Rings: The Two Towers, where real-life actors, landscape miniatures, virtual characters, and computer-generated backgrounds are all part of a single scene. The rendered shot is created and then divided into the various components which are used as exact guides for recording the pieces. Having this kind of video template makes post-production that much easier.

Production

Hollywood movies have traditionally been recorded to celluloid film by cameras. This adds a certain expected flavor to the scenes, but it involves a lot of manual editing in post-production. Recording live action straight to digital cameras is now possible on a professional level, as the costs for high-end digital cameras become more affordable every year. In addition, having all the material handy in digital format ready for digital post-processing application saves time in this latter phase. Many movies, from independent to blockbuster, are now being recorded entirely in the digital domain.

Post-production

Film post-production is where computer technology is most commonly used.

Digital Editing

Using a software interface to edit film has changed the task much in the same way that it has changed audio editing. Edits can be saved at various points, so it's easy to go back to a place where a destructive change was made. Edits can be played as soon as they are made, instead of after the film is prepared for projection. Files can be copied and shared with other members of the editing team.

But most importantly, the high-end tools used by the professionals can be scaled down for amateur use. Free, entry-level software like Apple iMovie or Windows Movie Maker allow the uninitiated to get their feet wet in digital movie editing, while products like Apple's Final Cut Pro or Adobe Premiere and AfterEffects make professional-quality editing and post-production affordable for the amateur or independent film-maker.

Rendering Farms

As mentioned many times previously, the power of the hardware available is often the only factor limiting what can be achieved by computer-generated special effects. The technology of distributed processing allows software to break through the confines of its hardware.

Distributed processing is where instead of sending all its calculations to one single processing unit, the software (or hardware) divides the calculations between many different processors so that these can process different parts of a command simultaneously, reducing the total amount of time required to complete a command. The more processors working on the same command, the less time it takes to be processed.

A "rendering farm", as it is known, is a customized network connecting multiple-processor computers, all using distributed networking to generate 3-D images and fuse them into finished video. Companies that do a lot of post-processing rendering, such as Pixar or Industrial Light and Magic, rely heavily on rendering farms to ensure post-processing projects are completed in sufficient time.

Digital Television

The media industry has been predicting for years that content-on-demand would be the future of television. For many reasons, the money needed to build a network infrastructure to support that type of entertainment delivery model has never quite been there, until recently. Pay-per-view digital cable and satellite television for on-demand movies or special events represent only the beginning of a trend towards leasing digital content-on-demand from the provider.

However, content-on-demand from the end-user's side is another recent trend that has caused quite a stir. Personal video recording (PVR) devices like the TiVo are both an electronic device and a subscription service at the same time. The electronic device is like a VCR, except that instead of video tapes, up to 80 hours of content can be recorded to a hard drive inside the machine. The subscription part provides access to TiVo's network of television listings and content database. Among TiVo's useful features are the "live pause", where you can press the Pause button during a live television show, and the TiVo will immediately start recording so that you can come back a minute later and resume as though the show were taped. Or, with digital cable or satellite subscriptions, some PVR devices can even record two shows simultaneously. Also, thanks to the subscription service for television listings, the TiVo can be programmed to selectively tape content based on certain parameters. For example, it can be set to tape every single new episode of your favorite TV series, but skip the repeats.

Some PVR devices, such as Sonicblue ReplayTV, even have features that allow the device to automatically skip commercials when recording. This move has angered many large broadcasting executives, because commercial advertising is crucial to the way their industry works. Businesses pay top dollar for ad time because they are guaranteed that a certain number of people will be seeing those ads. The broadcasters say devices to edit commercials out of televised content is "stealing". The electronics companies producing devices like ReplayTV, as well as privacy and users' rights advocates such as the Electronic Frontier Foundation (EFF) say that every user has the right to use their recording device any way they see fit. How do you see PVRs like TiVo and ReplayTV changing television?

4

COMPUTER TECHNOLOGY in
Law & Law Enforcement

- Introduction
- E-filing
- VR and Computer Assisted Simulation
- Biometric Identification
- Forensics
- Law Enforcement Technology
- Intellectual Property

Introduction

Cutting-edge technology has significantly impacted the legal system and all its many branches. Its effects are far reaching, and can be felt in fields that range from law enforcement to intellectual property. In order to appreciate the changes that technology has brought to these areas, it is necessary to learn a little about each and then look at specific changes brought about by recent innovation. These developments are not without controversy, and are often accompanied by serious concerns over how they affect the very individuals that they are supposed to protect and benefit.

E-filing

The current legal system is largely based on the filing of paper documents, a practice that has evolved over the course of the last few centuries. The administrative burden and expense of maintaining such systems is extremely high. As increasingly complex regulations, rules and legal procedures are put into place, greater and greater quantities of paper are required to evidence legal transactions. For example, lawyers in private practice are typically required to keep their paper client files in storage for as long as ten years after a matter is resolved and the file has been closed. This necessity can result in inconvenience, expense and storage difficulties.

Electronic filing, or e-filing for short, is a relatively new idea that has been increasingly tested and implemented over the last several years. With the proliferation of Wide Area Network (WAN) systems and the Internet, it is very feasible for a variety of legal documents to be electronically filed with centralized courts, government agencies and administrative organizations. This not only increases the ease of compliance with filing and limitation dates, it also relaxes the burden on traditional mail, courier and hand-delivery services.

A recent example is the Food and Drug Administration (FDA)'s move toward e-filing. Although the FDA has yet to make the electronic submission of documents mandatory, it has instituted a program of e-filing designed to allow it to more efficiently monitor and regulate the burgeoning pharmaceutical and biotech industries. These industries are already highly reliant on technology and automation, so the move towards electronic compliance is a natural step forward. This in turn will better enable the FDA to meet the health and safety challenges of the new millennium.

Another development points toward the creation of the electronic infrastructure necessary to accommodate these new electronic filing options. Software magnates Microsoft and BearingPoint recently teamed up to create a system for Texas courts that allows for e-filing of documents by lawyers. A reduction in time and cost, plus enhanced efficiency, are being touted as the benefits of the new system.

Ultimately, courts and administrative bodies will likely require e-filing or at least create strong incentives for it. Commentators have pointed to the airline ticket system, which encourages consumers to purchase e-tickets by offering them discounted cost compared with paper-ticket purchases, and to the banks, who charge greater fees for cheque processing than for many electronic payment alternatives. The day may soon arrive when those filing paper documents are charged user fees. Such fees will have the two-fold objective of discouraging an antiquated method of document management, while at the same time providing a means to pay for the new technology required to make e-filing a universal practice.

The move towards e-filing will need to be accompanied by increasingly reliable and comprehensive back-up and security systems in order to allay public concerns about the loss or theft of data. Lawyers and administrative organizations still tend to favor paper documentation because of the intangibility of electronic data storage. Indeed, the move towards larger and faster hard drives for data storage has been accompanied by an increasing degree of fallibility - hard-drive failure and loss of personal data is on the rise. However, this is balanced by an array of reliable back-up options that are cheaper and more powerful than ever before. Security is the other main concern. Firewalls and encryption systems ensure that the data in electronic documents can be viewed only by authorized personnel and cannot be intercepted or extracted from databases by unauthorized third parties. The quality and widespread use of these technologies will be key to creating a public confidence level that data is at least as safe in computer databases as it was in its old paper form.

Accessibility of Information

The move by government agencies toward digital and online formats has enhanced general access to such information by the public. Statutes like the Electronic Freedom of Information Act Amendments require many government records to be published online or made available in other digital formats (see below). When coupled with the proliferation of Internet access in the U.S., this translates to greater access than in the past when individuals would have to resort to mail or attend in person at government offices to view and copy documents of public record. Some judicial commentators have even expressed concern over the potential ease of access by members of the public to such items as court documents, citing the potential abuse of such information by individuals seeking to publish it for unscrupulous purposes.

VR and Computer Assisted Simulation

Virtual reality environments and computer simulations represent a relatively new technology that has emerged in the last quarter century. The increased processing speed and graphical rendering capabilities of modern computers has made it feasible to create increasingly realistic portrayals of real-life crime scenarios. The impact of this technology is far reaching, and it is employed in a broad range of industries, from engineering and architecture to computer graphic rendering of special effects in Hollywood movies. Computer modelers use photos, drawings and diagrams to create a virtual environment simulating a crime scene. This allows parties to move through a rendering of the original scene and study the location of evidence before it was disturbed.

Accident Reconstruction

The field of accident reconstruction in civil and criminal cases is a natural fit for computer recreation of real-life occurrences. It typically involves the use of computer simulation tools and expert testimony. This is characteristically in the form of 3-D animations, programmed to realistically depict the accident scenario. A variety of software products is available in the market place, most of which is specifically designed for engineering firms studying accidents in an effort to improve product safety and design. These products are commonly referred to as forensic animation and simulation software. The tools have been adapted to the courtroom because they can provide realistic depictions of accidents, which can be shown in real time or slow motion, paused, rotated, etc. This allows for a communication of crime scene details far beyond the simple diagrams or 2-D representations of the past.

Courtroom Simulation and Expert Testimony

An important aspect of any simulation system is its fidelity to the real-life scenario that it is intended to depict. Accident reconstruction typically involves experts who can generate the animations and testify to their accuracy. Although these software tools are available to the public, they typically require a degree of expertise to utilize and interpret. Expert witnesses are an important part of this process. To judges and juries they provide detailed explanations of both the physics and the engineering involved in the actual accident, and of how the software has been configured to accurately model these real-world dynamics. Having an expert on the stand is also a way for opposing parties to test the quality of the modeling through cross-examination of the expert responsible for providing this service. The ability to question the experts who prepare these simulations is an essential part of the process. Models and recreations will always contain shortcomings and simplifications. Opposing parties must be given opportunities to make judges and juries aware of the limitations of this technology as it portrays the real-life incidents of their case.

Although readily available to plaintiffs and defendants, the services of accident reconstruction firms have typically been limited to defendants with deep pockets or to high-profile government cases. This is because the technology has been cost-prohibitive until recently. This fact has raised concerns about the fairness of their use, given that these tools are available only to a particular segment of society able to afford them. However, the increased power and decreased cost of computer animation in general is quickly making this constraint a thing of the past. It is anticipated that even more sophisticated virtual reality-based reconstructive systems will soon be available to both investigators and litigators. These new tools promise to be far cheaper and much more powerful than their predecessors, opening new doors in our ability to understand the legal ramifications of real-life physical events.

Biometric Identification

Biometrics is an interesting new field that is being increasingly utilized by law enforcement officials on the local, national and international level. Biometric analysis concerns the use of high-technology tools to identify individuals. Traditional practices include fingerprint and signature analysis. New biometric technologies involve identification of the face, iris, retina, DNA and voice. While these recognition systems are often of obvious benefit to law enforcement officials, there is a legitimate public concern about the type of Orwellian "Big Brother"-dominated society that could result if these tools are misused.

Biometrics' most common large-scale use is negative identification. An example would be verifying that a person boarding a plane or entering another country is not a criminal offender . Another example would be using biometrics to avoid issuing multiple driver's licenses to the same driver. Biometrics is currently less useful for positive identification, wherein the goal is consistently correct identification of a particular individual over time.

Types of Biometric Identification

Facial Recognition

Face recognition relies on algorithms that represent the proportions of a person's face as a set of mathematical values. These values are based on the number of facial attributes scanned. The fewer the number of attributes, the faster a search through a database can be performed but the greater the chance for false hits. Conversely, a scan with a higher number of attributes will be time-consuming, but will achieve greater accuracy in the long run. In general, facial recognition is an evolving technology that is currently not very accurate. Facial recognition has applications in custody settings and non-invasive monitoring, such as video surveillance.

Iris Recognition

The patterns in the colored portion of the eye are essentially unique to each individual, making iris identification a highly accurate recognition technology. It is also well suited to large database searches. However, the high number of identifiers required for the data requires extensive cooperation from the individual being scanned. Iris scans have applications in access control technology, essentially allowing or limiting access to physical areas on the basis of recognition.

Fig.4.1 Retinal scanning at work.

Retinal Scan

Retinal scans rely on the unique arrangement of blood vessels at the back of the eye as the key identifier. The resulting process is similar to iris scans, while suffering the same limitation in that a high level of compliance is required from the person being scanned. Retinal scans also have an application in access control technology, allowing or limiting access to physical areas on the basis of recognition.

Fingerprints

Modern-day fingerprinting is based on a mathematical encoding of the link between the ridge endings/minutiae and ridge counts on the ends of particular fingers. This information is then compared with other fingerprint encodings on a database. This is a very accurate and widely-used system. Fingerprinting is commonly used as a crime-scene identifier and in custodial settings.

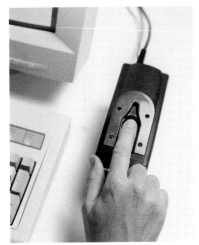

DNA

Each person has a unique pattern of chemical sequences at the genetic level that can be used as a very accurate identifier. Laboratory analysis of bodily tissue from the subject is typically required. This can lead to ethical issues about the invasiveness of forcibly taking samples for DNA evidence purposes. DNA can be used to identify either the victim or the perpetrator in a criminal setting. The evidence

Fig.4.2 Fingerprint scanner.

itself usually originates from the crime scene; subsequent tests are used in an attempt to place an individual at the crime scene.

Voice Pattern Analysis

Vocal characteristics are digitally recorded and then algorithmically analyzed for unique dynamic, harmonic and frequency characteristics. Background noise and normal voice alterations due to age can result in reduced accuracy, however. Voice pattern analysis can be applied in situations like telephone surveillance and access control technology.

The FBI's Combined DNA Index System Program, CODIS

The FBI's COmbined DNA Index System (CODIS) is an excellent example of a national strategy to use DNA evidence to resolve crime. CODIS is a computer-based system that is designed to match offender and crime scene information in order to identify serial offenders. Enforcement officials enter descriptions of biological evidence found at crime scenes into two indexes. The Forensic Index contains DNA profiles from crime scene evidence. The Offender Index contains DNA profiles of individuals convicted of sex offences and other violent crimes. The system allows police in various jurisdictions across the U.S. to share leads and coordinate their investigations. Once a match is made, DNA analysts in the respective laboratories contact each other for the purpose of validating or refuting a match. Parallel legislation in many states currently mandates the collection, storage and indexing of blood samples collected from convicted offenders in state DNA databases.

While the usefulness of these systems to law enforcement officials is obvious, there are some serious ethical and practical issues that arise. The invasiveness of collecting tissue samples from people accused of crimes is hotly debated, although most commentators will concede that sample collection from convicted offenders is less contentious. While the science behind DNA evidence is often assumed by the general public and law enforcement authorities to be virtually irrefutable, exceptions are beginning to surface. A recent probe of an FBI lab unit by the Justice Department's Inspector General provides a disquieting example. A forensic technician in the FBI lab failed to follow required procedure when analyzing DNA evidence over a two-year period. The length of time it took to detect the wrongdoing and the potential impact of the behavior both point to the potential fallibility of systems like CODIS. Clearly, a very high standard of conduct and procedure for laboratory personnel is required if this system is to be used to link individuals to serious offences and prosecute them.

The flip side to this is the use of DNA evidence to exonerate innocent individuals languishing in custody for crimes of which they have been convicted but did not commit. DNA evidence has been the key to freeing many individuals wrongfully convicted and sentenced to jail based on tenuous evidence such as erroneous eyewitness testimony, coerced confessions or poor legal representation. The evidence is often privately commissioned by the families of these individuals and non-profit organizations whose mandate is to investigate and act on claims of wrongful conviction. The availability of this technology to rectify injustice is a double-edged sword. On the one hand, it reveals the flaws of the justice system by illustrating how frequently this system sentences innocent individuals to prison, often for heinous crimes. This can erode public confidence in the fairness of the justice system. On the other hand, the very fact that DNA evidence is available as a highly accurate means to correct errors in the justice system should, in the long run, increase public confidence in the system as a whole.

Forensics

Forensics is the art and science of legal argument. Essentially, forensics is the study of the "science" behind the law.

Computer Investigations and the Law

Computer forensics is a recent field that is gaining increasing attention. This is a practice in which experts use computer analysis and investigation to obtain evidence. Types of crimes for which evidence is sought commonly include: computer crime/misuse, theft of trade secrets or intellectual property and fraud. This evidence exists in the form of data, typically stored on hard drives in the offender's computer. The recovery of deleted or damaged files as well as decryption, are often integral to the success of these efforts. Experts are frequently required to testify about the methods of data recovery and the quality of the evidence extracted from the offender's computer system.

Table 4.1 Application of Computer Forensic Evidence

Criminal Prosecutions	homicides, financial fraud, drug and embezzlement record-keeping and child pornography
Civil Litigation	fraud, divorce, discrimination and harassment cases
Insurance	fraud in accident, arson and workman's compensation cases
Corporate Law	sexual harassment, embezzlement, theft or misappropriation of trade secrets and other internal/ confidential information
Individuals	in support of wrongful termination, sexual harassment or age discrimination claims

IACIS® and the Standardization of Computer Investigative Procedures

Standardized forensic examination procedures have been established by organizations like the International Association of Computer Investigative Specialists (IACIS®). IACIS® maintains a standard for computer science in forensics. It comprises federal, state, local and international law enforcement professionals. Members follow a careful step-by-step procedure that is designed to help identify and retrieve evidence on the subject computer system.

The DEA Computer Forensics Program

The Drug Enforcement Administration (DEA) has a comprehensive Computer Forensics Program aimed at collecting relevant evidence in drug-related offences. Drug traffickers rely on desktops, laptops and hand-held computers to store the following types of information:

• Bank account numbers
• Names and addresses of associates
• Databases of assets and financial activity
• Sales and other business records
• Grid coordinates of clandestine landing strips
• Recipes for methamphetamine manufacture
• E-mail and other correspondence

Retrieval of such information while working in the field can offer great assistance in the investigation and prosecution of drug-related offences by the DEA.

The field of computer forensics raises issues of privacy and the protection of individual data. Individuals increasingly rely on computer data storage for personal information, media, work-related information, etc. Such data is stored in a range of devices including personal computers, laptops, PDAs, cell phones, and even devices like digital cameras and DV-cams. The increasing ability and willingness of the arms of the state to intercept, seize and use this data against citizens is an area of serious public concern. One way this is being addressed is through the creation and revision of privacy laws on a local, national and international scale. See below for a detailed discussion of privacy laws as they relate to this issue.

Law Enforcement Technology

New technology has impacted law enforcement considerably over the last two decades. Key innovations permit dispatchers to better coordinate police efforts and allow officers enhanced communication with one another. In addition, police units have direct access to all the essential information they need when en route to a call.

Computer-aided Dispatch: The Philadelphia Police CAD system

The Philadelphia Police Computer-Aided Dispatch (CAD) system is a model for any police department incorporating this technology into their dispatch system. CAD is a system that increases the efficiency and accuracy of the traditional police dispatch process. Dispatchers are essentially intermediaries between the public and the officers on the force. A dispatcher receives information about incidents from the public, assigns a priority to the call and then nominates police units based on their proximity to the location of the destination.

Under the CAD system, dispatchers receive information from 9-1-1 calls which they then input into a computer workstation. The following outlines the key features of the Philadelphia CAD system:

Table 4.2 Computer-aided Dispatch Procedure

1	A call is received by the call-taker.
2	The call-taker enters the information into specific fields of an online form.
3	The form is designed to differentiate and accommodate walk-in and on-site calls.
4	The call is assigned a priority rating that is continually updated.
5	The computer checks the validity of the address, dispatches it to broadcast units and assigns available police units.
6	Police notify the dispatcher through radio or mobile data terminal (MDT) when they arrive on the scene.
7	The computer automatically generates case/incident numbers for all assignments.
8	The system can be used to generate reports on complaints, dispatches and control vehicle activity.
9	Commanders can access an automated status board for each district on their terminals. It lists all vehicles working on a specific tour, their status and current assignment.

The CAD system allows fewer personnel to accommodate a larger call volume, track key pieces of information, prioritize calls and follow up with police units assigned to calls.

Technology in Squad Cars - MDTs

Mobile Data Terminals (MDTs) have existed in some form since the early 1980s. These specialized systems consisted of a proprietary computer system in a squad car with a very small display. While useful, these systems were expensive and difficult to deploy, with limited data transmission capability and no graphics.

In the 1990s the technology moved forward considerably. The mobile data industry evolved to include consumer products like pagers, cell phones and PDAs. A greater range of MDT providers meant that police no longer had to rely on the handful of companies that had formerly been the only options.

The present generation of MDTs is benefiting greatly from a communication industry driven by the public desire for higher-bandwidth wireless systems. In order to remain competitive with these public network systems, suppliers of MDT technology will continue to upgrade their existing systems. There is also the distinct possibility that large wireless phone providers will move to include public safety data as part of their offerings. It is likely that the next generation of products will use WLANS based on the high-speed data transmission Wi-Fi standard. In any event, new MDT units will continue to expand their practicality through enhanced data transmission and graphic capability.

Current MDTs handle a range of data that police officers rely on every day. They allow officers to receive data about individuals identified when making a traffic stop or going to a call. Since this data is available without the need to go through a dispatcher, there is the dual benefit of direct access to information and the ability to receive that information without alerting suspects. Officers can also message one another and let dispatchers know when they have arrived on the scene. More sophisticated applications include the ability to upload reports to supervisors, something that is often difficult to do with current technology, but a practice that will become increasingly common as newer systems come into place.

GPS/GIS Technology

Global Positioning Systems have become increasingly available in the last decade. Public-use versions are available as hand-held mapping devices and are often included as an option in new vehicles. These devices allow users to determine their location, accurate to the nearest meter. Systems in use by military and government agencies map to even higher accuracy levels. Geographic Information Systems are a related technology that allows for the plotting of destinations on detailed maps, including automated route planning.

Police agencies have begun to utilize both GPS and GIS systems. GPS assists officers in determining their precise location and plotting that against information about the location of incidents or suspects on the move.

GIS systems help to replace outmoded push-pin style maps that are commonly associated with the police investigation of serial crimes. GIS can easily generate graphic representations of data such as called-for services, arrests, field interview cards, citations, chronology, and officer data. On its own, this data is often difficult to visualize. Investigators can utilize GIS-based systems to quickly generate a variety of crime maps that can assist them in making helpful insights into cases.

The automated routing features of GIS systems are also very useful to accelerate police arrival time for incidents in emergency situations. Automated routing can also be used to enhance the planning and organization of mobile police units in non-emergency scenarios.

Intellectual Property

Intellectual Property is an area of law that has perhaps attracted the most controversy in recent years. The software and music industries in particular are locked in an on-going battle with digital piracy. Proponents on both sides have raised compelling arguments in an issue that has become increasingly complex and often misunderstood. In order to appreciate some of the issues of the copyright controversy, it is necessary to appreciate the key elements of intellectual property in general.

Definition

Intellectual Property is the law of ownership rights over products of the human intellect that have some value in the marketplace. The product typically possesses the characteristics of being unique, novel and unobvious. While ideas themselves cannot be considered intellectual property, the manifestations of ideas can. There are three essential areas of the law that deal with intellectual property: copyright, trademarks and patents.

Copyright Protection

Copyright is a form of legal protection afforded by Title 17 of the U.S. Code and the Copyright Act. Examples of the type of works protected by copyright include:

- Written and literary works.
- Music (composition, publishing and recording).
- Film, video and television.
- Visual art, graphics and photography.
- Computer software

Copyright occurs automatically upon creation of the work. Publication or registration is not required for a work to be protected by copyright law, although there can be certain advantages conveyed by these processes. The U.S. copyright office has a copyright registration procedure that helps to protect the rights of registrants.

The rights of copyright holders typically extend to their ability to do and authorize the following

- Make reproductions of the work.
- Prepare derivative works.
- Distribute copies or recordings.
- Publicly display the work.
- Publicly perform the work.
- Perform the work publicly by means of digital audio transmission

Copyright generally endures until the end of the author's life, plus an additional 70 years.

Peer-to-Peer File Sharing

Perhaps the most obvious controversy over the application of copyright law has arisen due to a phenomenon known as peer-to-peer file sharing. It has been practically possible to connect two or more computers via their modems in order to share data since the late 1970s. However, it is the recent proliferation of high-bandwidth Internet connections that has made public participation in mass file sharing a real threat in the eyes of copyright holders.

The issue arises because virtually any home user with an inexpensive personal computer and a high-speed Internet connection can download and use one of a variety of free peer-to-peer file-sharing programs. These file-sharing programs allow users to share any files on their computer with all other users connected via the same software program. Users can execute specific searches for various types of files which typically include music, movies, photos, software and electronic books. Once a user has found a file they are looking for, he or she can download it for free, often from multiple users.

The most outspoken opponent of this type of sharing has been the music industry, through its trade organization the Recording Industry Association of America (RIAA). When millions of users world-wide began sharing MP3s of music with each other, the RIAA member companies began to complain of a serious loss of profit. The RIAA began using its considerable financial clout to launch lawsuits against file-sharing services in an effort to shut them down. These actions put an end to a number of services based in the U.S., most notably Napster, Morpheus and Audiogalaxy. However, many file-sharing services based outside the U.S. continue their operations, much to the chagrin of the RIAA and its members.

The RIAA's argument is essentially that downloading music for free rather than paying for it is outright theft and is a breach of applicable copyright laws. It cites the high cost of producing and distributing music plus the fall in CD sales over the last three years as the evidence that file-sharing is ravaging the music industry. Opponents of the RIAA argue that the music industry has enjoyed an inflated price structure for years while putting out mediocre product and stifling creativity by tightly controlling the promotion, sale and distribution of music. Regardless of the many views on the topic, it seems quite clear that under the provisions of American copyright law, downloading music rather than paying for it is a breach of copyright that can clearly be prosecuted under the law.

The more difficult question for those seeking to stop peer-to-peer file sharing is practicality. It is practically impossible to identify and sue the millions of individual users who utilize file sharing services. Even if it were possible to identify such users, a plaintiff would have to gather evidence of illegal activity for each user. Further, actions against users in jurisdictions outside the U.S. raise conflict of law issues that become complex, time consuming and expensive to resolve.

The RIAA has taken the approach of initially striking file-sharing entities whose services were based on a centralized server. It then went after services that originated in the U.S. A more recent development has been the suit of Internet Service Providers (ISPs) to provide the evidence against users of those services to the RIAA for the purposes of their copyright infringement suits. The latest step is an attempt to identify and sue individual users whom the RIAA has identified as the worst offenders, those who routinely share thousands of copyright-protected works on their home computers.

Other industries have been similarly impacted by peer-to-peer file sharing. Software piracy has been an issue for software companies for well over two decades. So-called "cracked" software is software that has been altered by computer hackers to defeat any copy-protection system built in by its manufacturer. These files are then shared on peer-to-peer networks so that illicit users can download, install and enjoy the benefits of the software without having to pay for it. Clearly this activity also constitutes a breach of the provisions of the Copyright Act, so software companies have a similar stake in the actions against peer-to-peer services.

Patents

Patents are also governed by the U.S. Patent and Trademark Office. A patent for an invention is the grant of a property right issued by the Patent and Trademark Office to the inventor. The right conferred by the patent grant is expressed in the negative, i.e. it is the right to exclude others from making, using, offering for sale, selling or importing the invention. A patent endures for a term of 20 years from the date on which the application for the patent was filed in the United States.

What Can Be Patented

Any person who invents or discovers any new and useful process (industrial or technical), machine, manufacture (articles that were made), or composition of matter (chemical compositions), or any new and useful improvement thereof, may obtain a patent.

Trademarks

Trademarks are another type of intellectual property that is governed by the U.S. Patent and Trademark Office. A trademark is a word, name, symbol or device which is used in trade with goods to indicate the source of the goods and to distinguish them from the goods of others. Trademark rights are generally used to prevent others from using a confusingly similar mark, but cannot be invoked to prevent others from making the same goods or from selling the same goods or services under a clearly different mark. Trademarks must be registered with the U.S. Patent and Trademark Office.

The Digital Millenium Copyright Act

Congress passed the The Digital Millenium Copyright Act (DMCA) in 1998 in an attempt to prevent piracy of copyrighted material such as movies and music on the Internet. The bill was originally supported by the software and entertainment industries, and opposed by scientists, librarians, and academics.

The DMCA:

- ·makes it a crime to circumvent copy protection measures built into most commercial software
- ·outlaws the manufacture, sale, or distribution of code-cracking devices used to illegally copy software
- ·permits the cracking of copyright protection devices to conduct encryption research, assess product interoperability, and test computer security systems
- ·provides fair-use exemptions for non-profit libraries, archives and educational institutions under certain circumstances
- ·limits copyright infringement liability of ISPs for simply transmitting information over the Internet
- ·obligates ISPs to remove material from users' Web sites that appears to constitute copyright infringement
- ·limits liability of non-profit institutions of higher education for copyright infringement by faculty members or graduate students using Internet services on their campuses
- ·requires that "Webcasters" pay licensing fees to record companies
- ·states explicitly that "[n]othing in this section shall affect rights, remedies, limitations, or defenses to copyright infringement, including fair use..."

A number of actions under the DMCA have led many to question whether this legislation is achieving its stated objectives. Critics cite recent cases as examples of the DMCA being used to justify monopolistic anti-competition practices, limit fair use and even stifle free speech. Examples of the fair use of copyright-protected materials include the creation of copies of copyrighted works by legitimate owners, and technical breaches for the purposes of education and research by members of non-profit organizations. Individuals engaging in fair use have traditionally been exempt from laws intended to punish breach of copyright.

A recent example of an action under the DMCA is the case of Lexmark v. Static Control Components. Lexmark alleges that Static reverse-engineered a chip on a laser toner cartridge designed for Lexmark printers. Static alleges unfair trade practices in its countersuit against Lexmark. Fair-trade advocates are concerned that manufacturers like Lexmark may take advantage of DMCA provisions and limit their competition through the deliberate inclusion of digital devices on their products.

Another noteworthy case is US v. Sklyarov and ElcomSoft, which resulted in a verdict applauded by critics of the DMCA. Adobe initially sued Russian programmer Dmitry Sklyarov under the DMCA, but dropped the action at an early stage because of negative publicity over the case. The Department of Justice then proceeded against ElcomSoft, the company for which Sklyarov worked. It alleged that they had developed a product to circumvent Adobe Software's eBook electronic document copy protection. The essence of the case was the awareness of key ElcomSoft executives that their actions constituted a breach of the DMCA. Courts decided that ElcomSoft did not knowingly breach the DMCA, and therefore ruled in its favor. The case was an embarrassment to the Department of Justice and is viewed as a victory by DMCA opponents.

A third case worthy of review is Felten et al. v. RIAA et al. The RIAA threatened Felten and fellow researchers under the DMCA for their planned release of a research paper describing the defects in the proposed Secure Digital Music Initiative (SDMI) watermarking and lock-down schemes for audio CDs. The threats caused the researchers to withdraw their paper from a planned conference. Felten sued the RIAA, alleging censorship and breach of freedom of speech rights. The suit ended with assurances to Felten from the RIAA, the government, and a federal court that the threats against his research team were ill-conceived and will not be repeated.

It is clear that the legal ramifications of bold new technologies affecting intellectual property are complex and will generate controversy for years to come. Many more cases will need to be brought before the courts in order to interpret the scope of new laws such as the DMCA. Decisions in these cases will need to pay heed to legitimate and fair use of tools and practices which might otherwise be considered unlawful, but which are on the whole beneficial to the public interest.

As our society moves toward an economy that is increasingly based on intangible products that are transmitted and used in digital realms, intellectual property will become a very significant area of the law. There is likely to be fundamental change in three essential areas: copy-protection, income production models and law reform. Copy protection will continue to evolve to provide better protection for the owners of intellectual property, although such protection is likely to always remain temporary. Businesses based on intellectual property products will likely alter their income production models to generate revenue from other aspects of their technology than the mere sale and distribution of their intangible products. Finally, law reform will help to ensure that new protection is provided for the owners of Intellectual Property. Such laws must afford reasonable safeguards without the consequences of restricting free speech or fair use for personal purposes and academic advancement.

Privacy Laws

The host of new technologies in law and law enforcement provide many public benefits, but also raise some very legitimate public concerns. One of the key issues at stake is the intrusion by the state and its agents into the private lives of individuals. Various privacy laws have been enacted to protect these rights, and many laws are now being drafted and amended to take new technologies into account. Common examples of the type of technology that invades personal privacy include:

- Identity cards
- Biometrics
- Surveillance of communications
- Internet and e-mail interception
- Video surveillance
- Workplace surveillance

Federal Privacy Act (1974)

This act protects individuals by regulating how and when all levels of government can request disclosure of Social Security Numbers (SSNs), and by requiring that SSNs be maintained as confidential by those same governments and agencies. It also gives individuals the right to review records about themselves, to find out if the records have been disclosed, and to request corrections or amendments of these records.

Computer Fraud and Abuse Act (1986)

This statute essentially targets illegal activities such as hacking into computers and extracting or altering data/applications, and the transmission of computer viruses. The Computer Fraud and Abuse Act makes activities designed to access a "federal interest computer" illegal. A federal interest computer is a computer used by a financial institution or by the United States Government. Illegal activities under this statute include knowingly accessing a computer without authorization, exceeding authorized access restrictions, or transmitting a harmful component of a program, information, code, or command.

Electronic Communications Privacy Act (1986)

The Electronic Communications Privacy Act (ECPA) protects the privacy of electronic communications between individuals. In essence, the ECPA prohibits unlawful access to and certain disclosures of the content of private communication. The act defines electronic communications as any transfer of signs, signals, writing, images, sounds, data, or intelligence of any nature that affects interstate or foreign commerce, transmitted in whole or in part by a wire, radio, electromagnetic, photo electronic or photo optical system.

Computer Matching and Privacy Protection Act (1988)

The Computer Matching and Privacy Protection Act of 1988 (5 U.S.C. 552a(o) et seq.) amended the Privacy Act by describing the manner in which computer matching involving federal agencies could be performed and by adding certain protections for individuals applying for and receiving federal benefits. The statute essentially states that information collected by a federal government agency for one purpose may be used for different purposes by another federal agency. It institutionalizes data-sharing among federal government agencies. The act ensures integrity and fairness in its process, but not necessarily privacy. So while it was intended to afford certain protections to individuals subject to federal matching practices, it ultimately eroded privacy to some extent.

Freedom of Information Act

The Freedom of Information Act (FOIA) was enacted to ensure that that the benefits of government information are made available to everyone. The FOIA provides specifically that "any person" can make requests for government information. Citizens who make requests may remain anonymous and need not explain why they want the information that they have requested.

Electronic Freedom of Information Act Amendments (1996)

The FOIA was significantly amended in 1996 to embrace the revolution in electronic data collection and communication. The term "records" was expanded to include those maintained in computerized/electronic formats. Most records created as of November 1, 1996 must be made available either online or in other digital formats such as CD-ROMs. Federal agencies (including EPA) were compelled to create an index of material previously released under FOIA and make that index available online by the end of 1999.

International Privacy Laws

At the heart of international privacy law is the recognition that privacy is a fundamental human right recognized in all major international treaties and agreements on human rights. Nearly every country in the world explicitly or implicitly echoes this in their constitution. Constitutions drafted in recent times include specific rights relating to the access and control of an individual's personal information. The Organization for Economic Cooperation and Development and the Council of Europe have served as a model for the majority of these laws.

There is a growing trend towards the enactment of comprehensive privacy and data protection acts around the world. Currently, over 40 countries and jurisdictions have, or are in the process of enacting, such laws. Countries are adopting these laws to:

- address past governmental abuses (such as in former East Bloc countries),
- promote electronic commerce, and
- ensure compatibility with international standards developed by the European Union, the Council of Europe, and the Organization for Economic Cooperation and Development.

A chief example is the directive on the "Protection of individuals with regard to the processing of personal data and on the free movement of such data." This Europe-wide directive was passed by the European Union in 1995 to provide citizens with a wider range of protections from abuses of their data. The directive also imposes an obligation on member states to ensure that the personal information relating to European citizens is governed by law when it is exported to and processed in countries outside Europe. This requirement has resulted in growing pressure outside Europe for the passage of privacy laws.

The integration of new technology and the legal system is an inevitable result of the times in which we live. In both law and law enforcement, technology has helped to create a system that operates with a degree of efficiency and accuracy that has simply not been possible in the past. Yet these many improvements come with concerns that new tools may allow the state to become too controlling and invasive in the lives of citizens. Ultimately, technological progress must be coupled with fundamental checks and balances. These must guarantee that the enhancement of the legal system and law enforcement by technological innovation is not secured at the cost of individual liberty and privacy.

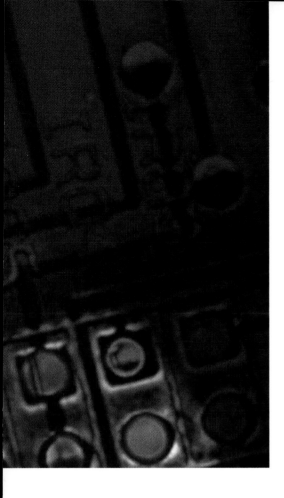

5

COMPUTER TECHNOLOGY in

A Potpourri of Emerging Technology

- OverviewOverview
- Trend Extrapolation
- Ergonomics
- Government Services
- Technology in Transportation
- What about Software?

Overview

This chapter focuses on the application of a variety of technologies which have touched our lives already, or will very soon. Many of these technologies or applications can have significant implications in our society and therefore can be controversial - both at a societal and at a personal level.

The purpose of this chapter is to identify some of these technologies (such as ergonomics, transportation, and government application of technology) and show how they are applied and how they can change our world, as well as raise some of the issues and challenges that can result from their use.

Trend Extrapolation

It's easy to predict the future, but the hard part is getting it right, particularly where technology is concerned. Past predictions don't offer much comfort. In 1876, a Western Union official said, "The telephone has too many shortcomings to be seriously considered as a means of communication. The device is inherently of no value." A century later, the chairman of a minicomputer corporation stated that there was no reason anyone would want a computer in the home.

Predicting the future will never be an exact science, but it's possible to approach the task in an organized way. In the field called future studies, scholars rely on a variety of methods to develop more accurate predictions. One method, called trend extrapolation, identifies current trends and projects them into the future. In this spotlight, you'll look at the trends driving contemporary computing, and you'll explore what may happen if these trends continue for the next several decades. You'll also examine the potential impact of artificial intelligence (AI), should computer designers succeed in creating a truly intelligent machine.

Tomorrow's Hardware: Faster, Cheaper, Connected

Could the history of the next 50 years be described simply by stating two laws of technology and economics? Consider these:

Moore's Law

Intel Corporation chairman Gordon Moore predicted more than 30 years ago that microprocessors and other miniature circuits would double in circuit density (and therefore in processing power) every 18 to 24 months. Moore's Law still holds true, and experts believe that the trend should continue for at least another decade, and perhaps for 20 more years, until the process of miniaturization of silicon components runs into physical barriers. If Moore's Law continues until the middle of this century, computers will be 10 billion times more powerful than today's fastest machines. Storage technology shows a similar trend: steep rises in capacity and steep declines in cost.

Metcalfe's Law

Ethernet inventor Bob Metcalfe predicts that the value of a computer network grows in proportion to the square of the number of people connected to it. Consider that a telephone line connecting two people is of limited value, but a telephone system that connects an entire city becomes an indispensable resource for every aspect of life. Under Metcalfe's Law, for example, a network with two people connected has a value of 4, but a network with four people connected has a value of 16. According to some predictions, the Internet will ultimately connect one billion users world-wide.

If you put these two laws together, you get a potent mixture: the computer industry is now giving us networked machines that double in power every 18 to 24 months, even as the networks they are connected to are rapidly growing in size.

As computers become faster, cheaper, and more valuable, they will encourage the trend toward the digitization of all the world's information and knowledge - the entire storehouse of accumulated human experience. And as digitization proceeds, the result will be increasing convergence among all media, communication, and networking technologies; the boundaries between telephones, newspapers, radio, television, and computers will fade away.

The Short Term

During the next several years, you'll see Moore's and Metcalfe's Laws at work. The table below lists the characteristics of a personal computer circa 2005, based on the assumption that Moore's Law will remain in effect. Besides these performance improvements, you'll see some basic changes in the standard PC's hardware, such as the use of flat-panel LCD displays in place of bulky cathode-ray tube (CRT) monitors. High-capacity, read/write optical drives will be standard equipment. New network technologies will bring megabit bandwidth to homes and offices.

Table 5.1 The Typical Personal Computer: 1999 and 2005

Component	1999	2005
RAM	64 MB	1 GB
Processor speed (instructions per second)	400 million	7 billion
Circuit density	7.5 million	125 million
Hard disk capacity	8 GB	135 GB
Average Internet connection speed (bits per second)	56,000	1 million

The Long Term

What will computing be like, several decades from now? By 2020, Moore's Law predicts that all the components of unbelievably powerful computers will be accommodated on just one tiny silicon chip, which can be mass-produced at a cost of $500 or less. These chips will include super-fast processors (capable of performing a trillion instructions per second), huge amounts of RAM, video circuitry - the works. And they'll cost less than $500. In some scenarios, they could cost as little as $100.

Recognizing the trends toward lower cost and miniaturization, some computer scientists speak of ubiquitous computing. (The term 'ubiquitous' means 'everywhere'.) In ubiquitous computing, computers are everywhere, and they fade into the background, providing computer-based intelligence all around us. Your car will inform you when it needs maintenance. Short on coffee?

Your pantry will automatically initiate an electronic order to the virtual grocery store, and a courier will deliver the coffee within minutes. You'll jot down notes on what appears to be a piece of paper, but everything you write will be automatically copied to a computer and then sorted and organized for storage. If you're missing a phone number you jotted down in haste, don't worry; it will be in your computerized address book. You'll wear computers, too. Tiny computers in your eyeglasses, for example, will adjust the lenses to light variations and display maps to help you find your way if you get lost.

The Limits of Trend Exploration

Like any method of predicting the future, trend extrapolation is only as good as the assumptions that underlie it. Moore's Law may break down if engineers encounter physical barriers to further miniaturization of electronic components; if so, future computers won't be as powerful or as inexpensive as trend extrapolation predicts. A second limitation of trend extrapolation lies in its failure to consider the impact of major technological breakthroughs, such as artificial intelligence (AI). If artificial intelligence is achieved, the future impact of computing will be far greater than trend extrapolation predicts.

Ergonomics

The physical work environment can have a significant impact on the health and well-being of office workers. Professional baseball pitchers and tennis players have long known that the repetitive action required in their sports can cause debilitating injuries (e.g., tendonitis, or tennis elbow) that can end their careers. Extensive mouse and keyboard use has been linked to a number of conditions relating to the wrist, fingers, back and neck. Repetitive Stress Injury (RSI) is caused by repetitive physical movements. One form of RSI directly linked to the repetitive finger motion when using a keyboard or mouse is carpel tunnel syndrome. This painful condition can prevent office workers from performing the basic functions of their jobs. Vision problems from frequent computer use have also been identified. Most computer users have experienced some form of eye problem, although in most cases this is minor.

In the 1980s and 1990s, computer and peripheral manufacturers gave little consideration to the long-term impact of repetitive use of computing devices. With experience and growing concern about injury, lost productivity due to absenteeism and the potential for liability, more attention is now focused on the design of computers and components to avoid known (and potentially future) health-related problems.

Ergonomics is the science of designing an individual's workspace to suit the needs of the individual. A greater emphasis is placed on the design for safe, comfortable and effective use. Workspace design includes everything from lighting, furniture, computer hardware and the placement of each of these components.

Ergonomics is much more than the design of seating or the design of car controls and instruments, as many people believe. It is the application of human scientific information to the design of products, systems and environments that are used for human activity. Ergonomics incorporates elements from anatomy, physiology, psychology and design, and applies them in ways that ensure that products and environments are comfortable, safe and efficient to use.

As new computer hardware is introduced, designers must be aware of the potential for injury due to repeated use. For example, new trends in mobile technology include the tablet PC and personal digital assistants (PDAs), which have the capability to add handwriting input or the use of very small keyboards. These may present new issues once we have the experience of repetitive use.

Other new technologies may help eliminate some of the problems associated with RSI. For example, voice recognition gives users the option of using their voice, rather than a keyboard, for the input of text. Wireless (e.g. infrared) technology opens up many new possibilities in the placement of keyboards and mice.

Another key component in the design of the safe, effective workplace is furniture. Elements such as chair height, seat-back angles and stiffness, seat angle, foot position, desk height and monitor position are all important considerations in reducing the risk of back and neck injuries.

Telecommuting - Advantages and Disadvantages

Many Americans have opted for telecommuting to avoid the daily grind of spending two hours a day (or more) in their cars. Telecommuters (or teleworkers) work at home either full- or part-time. With some level of coordination, part-time telecommuters can share office space with their peers, reducing the need for office space. In order to be effective, telecommuters need to have at home all of the necessary tools to conduct business as required for their job. This can include fax, an Internet connection (usually high-speed), a business phone line and voice mail. Telecommuting has pros and cons, both for the individual and for their employer.

Table 5.2 Advantages and Disadvantages of Telecommuting

	Advantages	Disadvantages
For Employee	More flexible work time	Limited social and professional interaction
	No commuting	Limited face-to-face contact
	More time for leisure, with family	Limited high-speed access in some areas
	Less stress	Concern about longer working hours
	Lower costs - clothes, fuel, food	Less visibility for promotion
For Employer	Less office space, lower costs	Difficult to measure productivity
	Less parking needed	Difficult to foster a team environment
	Happier employees, lower turnover	More complex technology issues

The primary motivation of telecommuting is to save time - a net gain of time by eliminating a daily commute can be applied to family time or work time, increasing productivity, employee job satisfaction (or both) and stress.

There is much debate on the effectiveness of telecommuting in employee productivity. Effectiveness depends on the type of work, the business office environment and the home office environment. The work habits of the individual also come into play, as some people have difficulty avoiding distractions at home (such as the refrigerator or pets) and separating home and business activities. Telecommuting applies primarily to office workers, who spend much of their time working at a computer or at a desk. Certainly, for professional athletes or entertainers, it's out of the question. And telecommuting certainly isn't for everyone. For jobs requiring a lot of interaction or team work, it may not be appropriate.

According to the Office of Personnel Management of the U.S. Federal Government, over 90,000 federal employees in 77 agencies took advantage of telework programs. This represents 14.4% of the employees eligible for telework programs, or 5% of the total federal workforce. This is a 20% increase over 2001 figures. As recently as 2001, the main barriers to adopting telework programs were management resistance and funding, indicating a lack of confidence by senior management in the ability of telecommuting to have a positive impact on organizational performance. This has recently changed - in 2002, the primary barriers were security and information technology-related issues.

There are a variety of societal benefits to telecommuting:

• Reduced automobile use

• Reduced energy consumption

• Reduced emissions

• Less traffic congestion

• Less capital spent on roads

In a recent study of 2,000 British Telecom telecommuters, 90% found they experienced less stress and increased their productivity as a result of telecommuting. And they had more leisure time.

The number of telecommuters in Europe has recently reached 20 million. According to the Office of National Statistics in the United Kingdom, the number of people in the U.K. who telecommute at least one day per week reached 2.2 million in 2002, or 7.4% of the entire workforce.

Government Services

Technology and Elections

The presidential election of 2000 in the United States raised some serious issues regarding the use of different voting technologies. Currently, there are five different voting technologies used in the United States: hand-counted paper ballots, mechanical lever machines, computer punch cards, marksense forms and direct recording systems (DRE).

Computer punch cards, marksense forms and paper ballots all use a physical ballot, whereas lever machines and direct recording systems require the voter to either pull a lever, push a button or touch a computer screen to cast their vote.

The table below outlines the use of the five systems in the U.S. in 1998.

Table 5.3 Use of Voting Systems in the US in 1998

	Characteristics	Percentage using this voting method
Paper Ballots	Paper ballot. No computer-assisted tabulation.	1.6%
Mechanical Lever Machines	No physical ballot - traditional recounts not possible. Introduced in 1892. Equipment no longer manufactured - declining in use. No computer-assisted tabulation.	18.6%

Table 5.3 Use of Voting Systems in the US in 1998

	Characteristics	Percentage using this voting method
Punch cards	First used in 1964. Physical ballot. Currently most common, but expected to decline. Can be computer-tabulated.	34.3
Marksense (optical scanning)	Introduced in the early 1980s.Includes physical ballot. Can be computer-tabulated.	27.3%
Direct Recording Electronic (DRE)	No physical ballot. Usage expected to increase. Can be computer-tabulated.	9.1%
Mixed System	Some jurisdictions used more than one method. It is not possible to distinguish the method actually used.	9.1%

Source: Election Data Services, "1998 Voting Equipment Study Report"

There are several challenges to upgrading voting systems in the US. The voting process is the responsibility of local and state governments. Each state legislature has established voting regulations, including voter registration, verification, monitoring, ballot handling, security, tabulation and recounts. There are over 10,000 election jurisdictions that administer federal elections. The capital cost of upgrading is beyond the means of many of these jurisdictions. For example, the state of Florida is considering the adoption of a DRE system for the 2004 election. The estimated cost is $200 million.

Upgrading the country's election process is a key initiative for the U.S. Federal Government and has become a hot issue due to the controversy surrounding the Florida election of 2000. Much was made of the "intent to vote" as a result of dimpled chads. A chad is the small piece of paper that is punched out of a punch card by the voter. A chad is considered dimpled when the paper was indented, but not punched out of the card. In the 2000 Federal election in Florida, the debate on the recount centered on whether the ballots with dimpled chads should be accepted as a vote, since it appeared that there was an intention to vote. Many believed that the majority of the dimpled chads would have been Al Gore votes. Counting these ballots as a vote, rather than a "spoiled ballot" could very well have tipped the scales in favor of the Democrats, putting Al Gore into the White House instead of George W. Bush.

Many democratic institutions around the world are wrestling with the same issues as the U.S. Brazil first introduced technology to the election process in 1990. Paper ballots were collected and entered by election workers for the tabulation of results. In 1998, Brazil conducted the largest electronic election in history. Over 60 million people (57% of eligible voters) voted electronically at polling stations (using a DRE system). Results were very quickly tabulated and published over the Internet.

Online Voting

There are several major hurdles that must be overcome before online voting will be adopted by the mainstream. These issues center on authentication, security and secrecy. Any system used must be able to positively identify each individual and to ensure they are a registered voter. Also critical is the security of the data - both to protect election results and to ensure that there is no way to determine how each person voted.

Online voting would be similar to DRE, in that the system will be electronic and will not include a paper ballot. This type of voting is very convenient for the voter, and as a result is expected to increase voter turnout.

Both DRE and online voting can reduce the number of spoiled ballots. Over-voting is caused when an individual makes more selections than allowed. Electronic voting systems will not allow this to occur. Electronic systems cannot prevent under-voting (not making enough selections), however they can reduce under-voting by providing visual (and audio) clues to the voter that additional selections are warranted.

U.K. Pilot Project

In May 2002, the U.K. government introduced new voting methods on a trial basis for 2.5 million voters (11.5% of the electorate). The trial included online voting and voting by mail. Voter turnout in the areas where the pilot was implemented was 38.7% compared to a national average of 32.8%.

On-line voting was conducted via the Internet, digital television, mobile phones (via text messaging) and touch-tone phones. Polling stations were also set up with touch-screen kiosks for those who prefer to vote in a more traditional location. There were no serious technology issues and no incidents of fraud reported. An additional, larger-scale pilot is being conducted in 200

Census

The U.S. Census Bureau is planning to conduct the 2010 U.S. census entirely without paper forms. The plan is to put 500,000 hand-held or mobile computers in the hands of their workforce to collect data electronically from 40 million American households.

While the details of the plan have not been finalized, the system would ideally use a combination of GPS and communication technology, and map and e-mail software, all designed to streamline the collection of data and publish the data sooner than otherwise possible.

Census data is critical for businesses to make strategic decisions. Millions of pieces of information are collected, organized and made available for organizations to use in ways that are relevant to them. There are many challenges. For example, the 2000 U.S. census contains 7 times the volume of data than the 1990 census.

Data storage, retrieval and compression technology make it possible to distribute this information in a practical and immediately productive form via CD-ROM, DVD and over the Internet.

Technology in Transportation

Telematics

Telematics combines wireless voice, data communications and Global Positioning System (GPS) technologies to deliver services to people in their vehicles. Telematics products and services can be classified into three areas: front seat - for safety and convenience; rear seat - for entertainment; diagnosis - to collect information on the operation of the vehicle.

These capabilities were first introduced in luxury models from several automotive manufacturers beginning with BMW and Acura in 1996. Original Equipment Manufacturers such as General Motors, Lexus and Daimler-Chrysler are committing to introducing telematics systems as standard equipment on more of their vehicles. In 2002, 20 automotive brands had offered navigation systems either as standard equipment or as an option on 72 models. Of all cars sold in the U.S. in 2002, 18% were equipped with navigation systems. The impact of these systems is

also having an impact on the used-car market, as consumers are prepared to pay a premium for cars equipped with these systems.

For the 2003 model year, General Motors' OnStar system is available in 53 models from 13 automotive manufacturers.

Some of the features of these systems include:

Remote control of vehicle functions

The ability of a call center to lock the doors, flash the lights or honk the horn on your vehicle - from anywhere in the country. The engine can also be immobilized remotely, should the vehicle be reported stolen. Police can then be notified of its position. It's possible to have the call center lock the doors with the thief inside. However, most thieves would likely break a window.

Integrated hands-free phone

Some systems incorporate a cellular phone, integrated with the vehicle. This can include fingertip control from the steering wheel, hands-free operation and voice-command technology.

Roadside assistance

With GPS technology and satellite communication, it's not necessary to let someone know where you are in order to get roadside assistance. The system can direct someone to help you, anywhere, any time. This capability can save lives in situations where the weather is particularly bad - for example, in a severe blizzard.

One-touch help

Systems like General Motor's OnStar system provide customers with an instant voice link to their call center, which can assist the driver on anything from roadside assistance to finding the nearest restaurant.

Driving directions

Systems such has the Hertz Neverlost system have been in use for years, providing visitors with detailed turn-by-turn driving instructions. Using a combination of Global Positioning System, a map system and a database of geographic features and other roadside resources, this system can pin-point a location to within a few yards.

Traffic conditions

New systems can also capture real-time traffic information to ensure you are on the best possible route, given current traffic conditions. This information can be reported to the driver, or used by navigation systems to provide alternate routes, avoiding traffic congestion.

Automatic emergency calling on air bag activation

Should the air bag deploy, an automatic call can be made to a call center, notifying them of the deployment, the vehicle description and the registered owner/customer. They can then initiate a voice call to ensure you are not injured. If you do not respond, the call center can immediately notify the police or highway patrol of your location.

Real-time diagnostics

If your engine or other components of your vehicle are malfunctioning (while you are driving), the manufacturer can be notified of the nature of the problem. You will receive a message that your vehicle needs maintenance and be given directions to the nearest authorized service center. If parts are required, these can be automatically ordered and shipped, either to the nearest service center for urgent maintenance or to your regular dealer.

Other features include integration with laptops and Personal Digital Assistants (PDAs) as well as access to information about your vehicle and your driving habits, and mileage information via the Internet.

Entertainment systems

Entertainment systems for the benefit of rear-seat passengers are currently available both from the dealer and from after-market vendors. Options include fully integrated systems with individual screens built into headrests, individual controls and headsets.

E-mail and Web access

The introduction of computers and Web access will result in a host of new services, including voice-activated Web searches, dictation, games, video and music on demand. Drivers will be able to send and receive e-mail and synchronize information with their personal digital assistants (PDAs).

Aside from all the benefits, these devices raises new social issues. For instance, if a driver is in an accident as a result of a distraction due to a telematicw device (cell phone, navigation system, audio system, etc.), who is at fault?

Application of (Front Seat) Telematics at BMW

There are over 50 million vehicles on Germany's 12,000 kilometers of motorway. Traffic congestion is a serious problem. Over 6 million breakdowns and 2 million accidents occur each year. BMW is designing its telematics applications for "intelligent traffic management".

The system in the vehicle communicates with 4,000 traffic-jam sensors on German roadways sending real-time information on traffic and road conditions.

In a specially equipped BMW X5, various sensors and communications systems ensure that the vehicle is notified about the current condition of roads and traffic. The system then notifies the driver. In heavy traffic, the driver can also "delegate" to the system acceleration and braking in stop-and-go traffic.

If the vehicle is approaching a sharp curve while on cruise control, the system automatically reduce speed. If not on cruise control, the system can provide an audio signal to warn the driver to reduce speed.

Crash Avoidance Systems (CAS)

Systems to avoid potential mid-air collisions have been in place on aircraft for several years. Similar technologies are being adapted for use in automobiles. The U.S. Department of Transportation's Intelligent Transportation Systems (ITS) research program into CAS has focused primarily on technology to deal with specific types of crashes, including rear-end, lane change, roadway departure and backing into another vehicle. Most of the emphasis has been on driver warnings, rather than automatic vehicle control. Adaptive Cruise Control (ACC) offers some degree of automatic vehicle control by providing limited braking and acceleration to manage the distance between vehicles.

Studies are under way to assess a driver's reaction to tactile signals (e.g., a vibrating steering column), audio warnings or automated braking by adaptive cruise control. This is critical to ensuring the technology is used as effectively as possible and that the systems reduce accidents rather than trigger them.

Pay-as-you-go Roadways

Taxes on gasoline are a form of user-pay system for drivers to use our roads. And there are many toll roads, bridges and tunnels where road maintenance and construction costs are paid by the users. However, the cost of toll collection is high - staff to collect tolls, equipment and security costs can consume a large percentage of the tolls collected. Many jurisdictions have implemented automated toll booths using technology such as smart cards to allow drivers to coast through the toll booth while fees are automatically deducted from their smart cards, or they are identified as monthly customers.

But with advances in information and communication technology, it is possible to charge users for actual usage, vary the fees by time of day, day of the week and even based on how crowded the road is at that moment. In theory, as fees rise, there will be fewer cars on the road. This latter concept was conceived by the late William Vickrey, a Columbia University professor and Nobel economics laureate. Not only would this constitute a true user-pay system, it would be an effective tool to reduce traffic congestion in major urban centers.

Congestion Pricing: Promises and Challenges

Many toll road systems have introduced automated toll collection, mainly to reduce the cost of collecting tolls and to reduce congestion at collection points. Congestion pricing takes the concept further and allows jurisdictions to vary the cost of using roads according to time of day, type of vehicle, volume of traffic, etc. As a result of advances in computer and communication technologies, it is now possible to build "smart" roadways, enabling the use of new pricing and toll collection schemes. Many variations on user-pay or pay-as-you-go schemes are being considered in many jurisdictions, both in the U.S. and abroad. And while it is now possible technologically, there are many legal and political hurdles, as was found by the city of London, England in the recent decision to introduce congestion pricing in its city center. The following are examples of how technology has been applied to solve traffic congestion, reduce pollution and reduce the cost of toll collection.

Electronic Road Pricing (ERP) - Singapore

To reduce the congestion in its downtown area, Singapore has introduced the ERP system, which collects tolls from vehicles entering high-traffic zones during peak times. As cars approach the toll zone, an electronic board displays the current toll charge, giving vehicles the opportunity to avoid the charge by staying out. A cash card may be purchased at a wide variety of outlets and attached to the windshield so that tolls can be automatically deducted as the vehicle passes under gantries.

As a result of the implementation of this system, traffic volumes were reduced by 13% during peak times and average traffic speed in high-traffic zones increased by 22%. The system has also resulted in an increase in car-pooling.

Alternative Transportation

The Segway

The Segway HT (Human Transporter) is a self-balancing transportation device for one person, designed to operate in a pedestrian environment. It allows people to commute, shop, and run errands more efficiently and with little effort. And it does it all by harnessing some of the most advanced, thoroughly-tested technology ever created.

Using a combination of five gyroscopic sensors and ten microprocessors, the Segway is controlled by simple body motion. Lean forward and the motor kicks in to move the vehicle forward. Stand straight and it slows to a stop. To provide stability, position sensors are checked 100 times each second and corrections are made to keep the Segway vertical.

The wheels are controlled independently, allowing the Segway the flexibility to turn on the spot.

The Segway has a top speed of 12.5 miles per hour, has a range of 17 miles on a single charge and weighs 80 pounds. It can carry up to 325 lbs.

They can be purchased on amazon.com for just under $5,000.

Driverless Transportation

Driverless transportation - that is, trains, large cargo trucks and small passenger vehicles, is a technology trend growing more common in urban areas with a high volume of short-range traffic.

In a nutshell, there are two main types of driverless transport: those vehicles that use rails to guide their path, and those that rely on sensors to navigate a dedicated roadway or space.

Rail-guided transport, like the driverless metro (subway) lines in Paris, Singapore, and Kuala Lampur, relies on rails to guide its path, and relies on sensors only to detect obstacles on the rails. The Meteor Line 14 in Paris, for instance, has high glass shielding separating the running line from the platforms at each station, to keep obstacles (and people) from getting in the train's way. The automated Meteor metro line cost 6.8 billion francs (about $1.3 billion), but was estimated to have relieved surrounding lines by about 8,000 passengers per hour. In addition to the construction of the lines and purchase of the automated rail systems and controls, these costs also included moving the location of one existing metro station and increasing access to others.

Sensor-guided systems have also been used in many driverless vehicles. Currently, the technology works best for short-distance, high-traffic routes. Yamaha, for instance, manufactures a driverless personal transport vehicle called the AGV (Automatic Guided Vehicle), which it successfully used in 2002 to provide transportation up and down the 1.2 km hill which was the main attraction in the Floriade horticultural show in the Netherlands.